D+ 247551

Championship Baseball Techniques, Fundamentals, and Drills

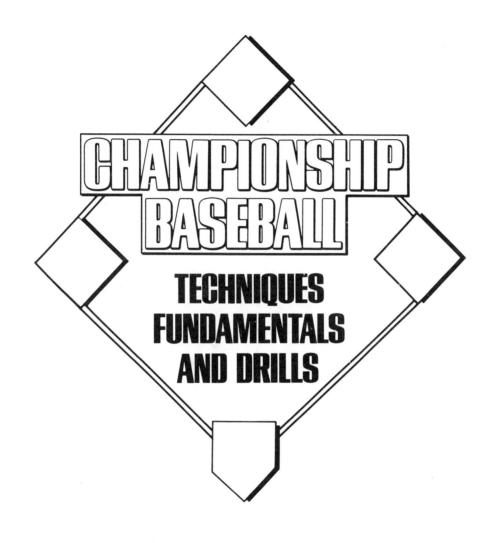

CHAMPIONSHIP BASEBALL

TECHNIQUES FUNDAMENTALS AND DRILLS

Joe Russo   Don Landolphi   Howie Gershberg

Parker Publishing Company   West Nyack, New York

© 1985 by

PARKER PUBLISHING COMPANY, INC.

West Nyack, N.Y.

Library of Congress Cataloging-in-Publication Data

Russo, Joe.
  Championship baseball techniques, fundamentals,
and drills.

  Includes index.
  1. Baseball—Coaching. I. Landolphi, Don.
II. Gershberg, Howie.
III. Title.
GV875.5.R87 1985   796.357'07'7   85-16765

ISBN 0-13-126178-9

PRINTED IN THE UNITED STATES OF AMERICA

Dedication

To our wives and children,
who have shared our wins and losses:

Cecelia, Joey, Christine, and Katherine

Rosemarie, Dan, Phil, and Michael

Theresa, Bob, Chris, John, Theresa, Jim, Debbie, and Cathy

How This Book
Will Help You

This book provides a systematic and organized approach to teaching the fundamental skills and techniques that are required to play the game of baseball. The best players enjoy not only winning games, but also developing and improving their own playing skills. Championship coaches derive deep satisfaction from watching players develop under their tutelage.

As a coach, you must assume that your players enter your program knowing virtually nothing about playing well, and that it is your task to teach your players everything they need to know. From the beginning, you must teach your players the importance of regular, enthusiastic practice and drills. You must convince every player that the team that masters basic skills becomes a well-oiled machine that will roll on to victory. Hard, careful practice is the base of a pyramid on which you build a championship team.

Hitting a home run, pitching a no-hitter, or making the game-saving defensive play are all satisfying accomplishments, but in order to be able to do these things, baseball players must put in hours of hard practice and work on fundamental skills and techniques. The way they practice is the way they will play in a game. In this book, we show you how "Perfect Practice Makes Perfect."

From thousands of practice sessions and hundreds of games, we've discovered the most effective drills for developing the skills each player must have. We've presented these in the order most coaches prefer for an organized program.

We start with a chapter on the fundamentals of pitching, with an emphasis on the "Essential Five Pitching Skills," and specialized drills to develop them, such as the Pivot and Rotation drills. You can follow the progression of such drills through a series of photos and illustrations that show the mechanics of pitching, along with the various grips used to throw the fast ball, curve ball, slider and change-up. You'll find that using these drills will make teaching pitching skills a much easier task. We also stress the importance of the pitcher as a fielder. Many fielding, fast-play drills are described, not only for the pitcher, but also for the catcher and infielders. And we discuss the relationship between the pitcher, the catcher, and the umpire.

Next, we describe the skills needed to become an outstanding defensive catcher, with special emphasis on stance, shifting, blocking balls in the dirt, and throwing. Many drills for the development of a fine catcher are presented. The "Art of Framing" is a special feature in this chapter.

In our chapter on hitting we show you an unusual theory that has proved very successful in coaching players on getting solid, base-producing hits. When your players thoroughly understand and apply the "Contact Spot" theory, they will have the power that wins game after game.

Proven strategies on baserunning and stealing bases are discussed in detail in Chapter 8. Here we show you successful techniques of stealing second and third base and what to look for in the opposing pitcher when attempting to steal a base.

The "crossover step" and the "toe-out" tricks of baserunning are fully explained and illustrated. Tips for coaching first and third bases are also given in Chapter 8.

In our chapter on Infield Play, we break down each position individually, describing qualifications, positioning, fundamentals of catching and throwing, and an overall knowledge of infield techniques.

"Double Play: The Pitcher's Best Friend" is an in-depth study of the many methods of making those crucial plays that take out two runners. We've placed particular emphasis on the pivots and feeds that the shortstop and second baseman will make during the course of the game. You'll find our drills break down the double play to its simplest form. And we've discovered that the "paddle" is an outstanding method of teaching a player to make the pivot. This "Paddle Method" is a gimmick all coaches will want to try.

The chapter on Outfield Play shows you a series of progressive drills that will help you to develop a strong, defensive trio of outfielders. Fast cutoffs, relays and all outfield situations are fully explained and illustrated.

We have taken the basic fundamentals, explained them in their simplest form, and then given you in each case a series of effective drills that will lead up to perfect execution of these fundamentals. This is not to say that a player who executes his part of a play correctly every time in practice will always execute it properly in the tense moments of a close game. Errors can't be completely eliminated—they're part of the game. Still, players who build a high level of skill in practice will consistently show that level in the games themselves. If players are conditioned mentally and physically to win through daily drills, they will be much better equipped to face the trials of actual competition. These techniques enable coaches to prepare their teams to meet all the situations that might arise during the course of a game.

With regular, consistent application of the techniques in this book, we're sure you will strengthen every player on your team and lead them to a championship season!

J.R.
D.L.
H.G.

Acknowledgments

We would like to acknowledge all those coaches and friends who have instilled in us a love of the game of baseball and who have inspired us to write this book. Former coaches, assistant coaches, and all of our former players have contributed to the many ideas put forth in this book.

Special Thanks to

 Jack Kaiser for being the coach and person he is.

 Mrs. Harriet Griffin for typing the manuscript.

 Ron Linfonte for his contributions in the area of training techniques.

 Joe Consentino, Cyril Morris, and Jeff Kollbrunner for their photography.

 Andrew and John Zaferes for their outstanding illustrations and diagrams.

Contents

Key Symbols

Note—The following symbols are used to illustrate the diagrams and drills used throughout the book:

1	—	Pitcher
2	—	Catcher
3	—	First baseman
4	—	Second baseman
5	—	Third baseman
6	—	Shortstop
7	—	Left fielder
8	—	Center fielder
9	—	Right fielder
INF	—	Infielder
OF	—	Outfielder
R	—	Runner
F	—	Fungo hitter
S	—	Shagger
HC	—	Head coach
AC	—	Assistant coach
M	—	Manager

-------------------------------------> Path of thrown ball

————————————————————> Movement of player

∿∿∿∿∿∿∿∿∿∿∿∿● Path of ground ball or fly ball

● — Baseball

■ — Base

PITCHING:
The Basic Mechanics
for Winning

Baseball experts estimate that pitching can be 50, 60, 70, 80, or even 90 percent of the overall defense of a team. Regardless of what value a particular team places on its pitching, there is no disputing how important it is for teachers, coaches, and the pitchers themselves to learn what factors make pitching successful. Your pitchers will achieve their best results by understanding and implementing the basic mechanics of their bodies and throwing arms.

Coordination of "arm and body" movement is essential. When your pitcher's arm and body are forced to work independently of one another, he loses all his mechanical advantage and the arm bears the brunt of the effort. Your goal as coach is to help your pitcher develop a good fast ball and breaking pitch, along with control. This is generally the result of a smooth, coordinated delivery, in which the pitcher maintains his balance and allows his arm and body to work together.

Successful pitchers have different styles of delivery. However, balance, hand speed, grip and ball rotation, weight retention, and a good follow-through are essential in all styles of throwing a baseball. A pitcher must be comfortable when throwing; when he finds that style which is best suited for him, he must work to perfect it. Only through constant practice can any pitcher hope to acquire a "groove" that will allow him to be in control of his pitches at all times.

General styles of pitching fall into the following "angle" categories. Pitchers who throw down at the hitter generally use an *overhand* or *three-quarter* angle. This permits the pitcher to use his full arm leverage and allows him to throw the ball on a vertical plane. This will break his curve down and cause his fast ball to ride up, up and in, or down and in. If the angle of the arm gets further away from the body than three-quarters, it will be difficult to break the curve ball down, forcing the pitcher to throw a "slurve" or slider as his breaking pitch. The young pitcher must find the most comfortable way of throwing and then apply the basic mechanics that will allow him to become as successful as he possibly can.

To find the most comfortable angle of delivery, position the pitcher in the outfield approximately 200 feet from home plate. Roll a ball directly at the pitcher. The pitcher should field the ball with two hands and throw the ball as quickly and as hard as he can to a catcher at home plate. This will allow both you and your pitcher to discover the most comfortable arm angle in which the pitcher can obtain power in his throw. For example, a three-quarter arm angle pitcher will throw from the three-quarter arm position (Photo 1-1). An overhand pitcher will throw directly over the top (Photo 1-2). Other pitchers throw side arm (Photo 1-3).

Photo 1-1

Photo 1-2

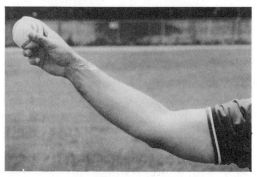

Photo 1-3

The height of the elbow in relationship to his shoulder is an important factor as it is coming into the release area. The height and the angle it makes with the shoulder should be determined by:

1. being comfortable
2. being at the release point that provides best movement and control

THE ESSENTIAL FIVE PITCHING SKILLS

Balance, hand speed, ball rotation and grip, weight retention and follow-through we call the "Essential Five Pitching Skills." The value of concentrating on the essential five is that it allows your coach and your pitcher to see what points need to be understood and what points may be used as cues and checkpoints in the learning process. Let's list the basics of the essential five.

1. Balance

It is important for a pitcher to maintain his balance throughout his delivery. A loss of balance will generally cause the pitcher to rush his body, resulting in an uncoordinated arm and body movement. A loss of balance can also throw the pitcher's head, shoulders, and hips off target, making it difficult for him to control his pitches. When the pitcher comes to the pivot position, he should be able to pause and look at the catcher's glove with his leg up and his lead shoulder and hip pointed toward the batter without falling forward or off to either side. A good way to check whether this occurs is to place the pitcher on his pivot and see if he can hold his balance for a few seconds.

2. Hand Speed

Hand speed is the time from the moment the throwing wrist begins to go forward until the ball is released. The greater the hand speed, the more velocity and spin the ball will have. Hand speed is increased as the pitching elbow is raised, which causes a fuller arm extension. The more the arm is extended, the more hand speed is obtained. Breaking the hands from the pivot vertically and above the belt will help straighten the pitching arm as it comes out of the glove, and also increases the momentum going into the power release areas. A full wrist snap and follow-through, along with a good grip in which the pitcher does not choke the ball, also will increase the hand speed.

3. Ball Rotation and Grip

The way the ball rotates controls the direction in which the ball will move. If a fast ball has back spin, it will rise. If a ball has overspin, it will drop (curve ball). Finger pressure can cause the ball to move in the direction the pitcher wants. Applying more pressure on the index finger and turning the ball over slightly will give him a sinking fast ball. Holding the ball slightly off center and allowing the middle finger to push the ball off the inside of the index finger will make the ball slide. Have your pitcher experiment with different grips to see which one gives him the best movement and control of his ball. In most cases when gripping the ball, the top fingers and thumb should be on a seam in order to get better spin on the ball. It is also important that the ball not be choked too far back in the palm as this retards the wrist snap. An exception would be when the pitcher wants to throw a change-up.

4. Weight Retention

Rushing the body, that is, shifting the body weight forward too soon, can be one of the biggest problems a pitcher will face. He must hold back or retain his body weight long enough so the pitching arm will bring it forward. Check that when the stride leg lands the pitching arm is up with the wrist loose and palm down. The upper body

Photo 1-4

should not be leaning forward until the throwing arm comes through, opening the front shoulder and bringing the body behind the pitch. Along with the thrust off the rubber, the hips must fully face home plate to allow the body weight to come through and generate power into the pitch.

When the body weight goes forward before the arm, the arm usually takes a shortcut to catch up. This results in short-arming the ball (dropped elbow), which causes a loss of hand speed and a cutting down of the downward flight of the ball (see Photo 1-4). Another problem that results from rushing is that the body gets too far ahead of the arm. This causes the arm to lag behind the body thus placing all the strain on the arm.

5. Follow-Through

Follow-through is important for speed and control and allows the pitcher to be in good fielding position. The body weight should be over a bent front knee and on the ball of the foot. The pitching arm should snap straight across the chest to a position alongside the front knee. This pitching against the resistance of the front leg gives the pitch its final snap. As the ball is released, the gloved hand should remain close to the side of the body with the palm facing out. The rear leg is carried forward and planted a comfortable distance to the side and a little ahead of the striding leg. This puts the pitcher in a squarer position facing the batter and ready for any ball hit toward him.

Before we get into the pitching delivery, let's talk briefly about the grip. This is the one aspect of pitching that is highly individualistic, but where a few general comments can be made that should help coaches and players.

THE GRIPS

The best grip is one that feels comfortable and gives the most movement. In most cases it is advisable to have the middle and index fingers along with the thumb on a seam. This will allow better control of the ball and produce a greater amount of spin. The middle and index fingers should be slightly hooked around the ball about ⅛-inch apart from one another. The thumb is straight and underneath the ball in the middle of the two top fingers. The rest of the fingers are alongside the ball. The three pressure points are the index and middle finger tips and the thumb joint. The ball should be held fairly loose and not in a choked position so the muscles in the wrist and forearm are not tense.

The Fast Ball

There are two ways to hold the fast ball—with the seams and across the seams. The ball should be held as far out in the front fingers as comfortable while still maintaining the ability to control the ball. The pitcher should try to achieve strong pressure on the finger tips along with a snapping down of the wrist to create spin that will cause the ball to move.

Holding the ball across the seams (Photo 1-5)

When gripping the ball across the seams, the two top fingers are at a point where the seams are farthest apart. The thumb is underneath resting on the bottom seams. When the ball is released with a vigorous wrist snap, it creates back spin on the ball causing it to hop or rise. Since four seams are rotating at once, it gives the ball a greater chance of moving in the direction of the spin. A pitcher who uses an overhand delivery will usually get the ball to move straight up because his fingers are directly behind the ball. A three-quarter delivery will generally get the ball to move up and into a right-handed batter because the ball will generally come off the outside of the middle finger causing it to slice or tail.

Photo 1-5

Holding the ball with the seams (Photo 1-6)

Pitchers who hold the ball with the seams generally get a sinking fast ball by turning it over slightly. Turning the wrist slightly to the outside causes the rotation of the ball to go downward into a right-handed batter. The ball is gripped with the two top fingers alongside the seams and the thumb underneath across the seams.

Each pitcher should experiment by holding the ball in different ways to see which grip gives him the most effective movement and control.

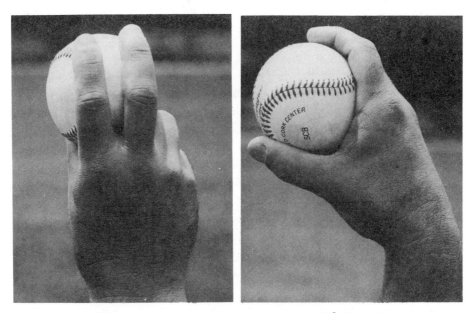

Photo 1-6　　　　　　　　　　**Photo 1-7**

The Curve Ball (Photo 1-7)

The curve ball is an effective pitch if it moves down or down and away from the bat. If it just breaks to the side, the ball remains in the hitter's contact zone for a longer period of time. It is also more difficult for the batter's eyes to adjust vertically than horizontally, making the pitch that moves down more difficult to hit. The curve ball is thrown with the middle and index fingers on top of the ball creating a pulling down action with the middle finger, which causes the ball to be released over the first and second joint of the first finger. This will create overspin and cause the ball to move down. It is advisable to hold the ball with the seams where the middle finger is across the front part of the seam and the thumb resting across the bottom seams. This will allow four seams to rotate as the ball comes out of the hand.

As the pitching arm comes forward, the elbow stays high and the wrist turns inward, which causes the palm of the hand to face the head. This puts the ball in a position from which it can be released with a rolling motion off the fingers. The pitcher should think "fast ball" until the arm is close to the head. The elbow is now leading and the wrist turns in and snaps downward with pressure from the index finger and thumb creating a rapid spin on the ball.

Problems that occur when throwing a curve ball include

1. *Overstriding*, which prevents a pulling down action with the arm
2. *Dropping the elbow*, which leads to short-arming the ball and causes the ball to hang
3. *Thinking curve ball too soon*, which causes the pitcher to wrap his wrist and lock it

Remember, think "fast ball" until coming forward, then turn and pull.

The Slider (Photo 1-8)

The slider is a late and quick breaking pitch which results from slightly cutting a fast ball. By making a one-quarter inward turn of the wrist or holding the ball off center like a football, it will leave the inside part of the index finger and rotate in a direction toward the outside part of the plate to a right-handed batter when thrown by a right-handed pitcher. The slider can also be used as a breaking pitch for a pitcher who cannot throw an effective curve because of his arm angle or wrist action.

Generally a slider is effective when thrown low and away or in on the hands. It is also a good pitch to throw when you are behind where the hitter generally zones for a fast ball.

The two most common ways of teaching the slider are the off-center method of holding the ball like a football and the one-quarter inward turn of the wrist. In both cases the middle finger applies pressure pushing the ball off the inside part of the index finger. The slight inward turn of the wrist causes the ball to act like a fast ball breaking at the last second—it is just the opposite action as a tailing fast ball.

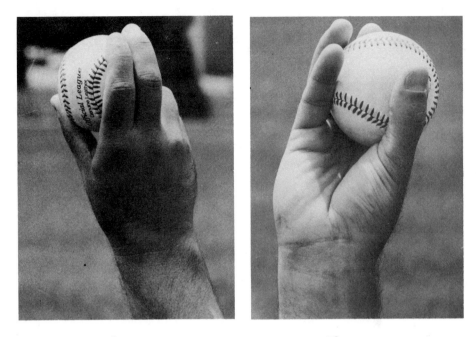

Photo 1-8   Photo 1-9

The Change-Up (Photo 1-9)

A change-up is a pitch that comes off the same motion and arm speed as a fast ball, but with less velocity. The most effective way of doing this is to retard the wrist snap so the ball does not have added speed.

There are a few different ways of teaching the change-up and a pitcher should experiment with each until he finds the best for him. One method is to place the ball deep in the hand with three fingers on top. As the ball is about to be released, the pitcher should lift the finger tips up and bury the heel as if he is pulling down a window shade. By removing the finger tips from the ball and locking the wrist, it slows the ball down. Another method is to place the ball back in the palm with three fingers on top of the ball. As the hand comes into the release area, let it roll off the fingers with a slight outward turn of the wrist. This will cause a slight tailing action with fast ball spin. It is also advisable to drag the pivot foot in order to slow down the body action.

Always try to keep the change-up low. We advise our pitchers to aim to almost hit home plate with the pitch, making them concentrate on a low target. The change-up allows the pitcher to upset the batter's timing and will fool him many times.

Once a comfortable grip has been found, the pitching delivery must be understood so the proper results may occur.

PITCHING DELIVERY

The pitching delivery begins when the pitcher steps onto the rubber to receive his sign and ends when he squares off after his follow-through.

The most important part of the delivery is when the pitcher gets into the pivot position where he is balanced. This is the checkpoint to make sure he has it all together before he explodes forward. The preliminary motion before the pivot is just a buildup to the power that will be applied when the pitcher will go forward and transfer his weight to his front leg. If a pitcher has problems that cause a loss of balance or concentration in the full windup, then a no-pump windup is suggested. This will get him into the pivot position without any wasted motion. For the pitcher who likes to build up his momentum and stretch his arms over head, we suggest the type of delivery outlined below. Everything here is geared to a right-handed pitcher, so all left-handers should visualize what they would do from their side.

Position on Mound When
Taking Sign with No Runners on Base

The pitcher should be erect or stand straight up (relaxed) with the right foot on the right side of the rubber with the front spikes just over the edge. The toe of the pivot foot points slightly out making it easier to rotate the body when going into the pivot. The feet are comfortably spread with the body weight balanced equally on both feet. The left foot is slightly behind and to the side of the right foot (Photo 1-10). The head, hips, and shoulders are square to home plate with the throwing hand in the glove about chest high or with the throwing hand to the back and side of the right thigh. After he takes the sign, the pitcher should take a deep breath, relax, and then begin the wind-up (Photo 1-11).

Windup (Photo 1-12)

As the pitcher steps straight back with the left foot, his hands swing over the head with the elbows slightly out. The ball should be well

Photo 1-10

Photo 1-11

Photo 1-12

hidden in the webbing of the glove so he does not allow the batter to pick up the grip, tipping off the pitch. At this point his head should remain still and looking straight ahead at the target. Some pitchers like to step to the side with the left foot making it easier to rotate the body. This will generally cause the head and shoulders to face toward the third-base side which makes the pitcher's first movement toward that side rather than forward. This is called pitching around the corner. By doing this his weight is moving toward the third-base side first, and there is a greater tendency for the pitcher to throw across his body. Actually, the pitcher should step straight back, keeping his head and shoulders square to home plate and just rotate into the pivot position.

Body Rotation (Photo 1-13)

As the hands come over the head, the ball of the right foot moves to the right, parallel to the rubber. The left knee is lifted and the hands come down to the height of the chest. At this point the body is rotated to the right with the lead shoulder and hip pointing directly toward home plate. Some pitchers like to position their pivot foot half on and half off the rubber to use it to get a better push off. Unless the mounds are well kept and the dirt around the rubber is hard, it is difficult for the pitcher to maintain his balance in the pivot position, especially if a deep hole has been dug in front of the rubber.

Photo 1-13

Hand Break

The hands should break fairly high in order for the pitching arm to stretch down and swing up. The break is actually a vertical break so the pitcher can get a swinging action and build up momentum going into the release area. An important point to remember is the more extension your pitcher can get with the arm, the more hand speed he will get. Also keep in mind that the wrist of the pitching hand should be loose and the palm pointing down until he actually starts his forward release of the ball. This will give him a whip type of action, applying more velocity and spin to the ball.

Photo 1-14

Photo 1-15

Lead Arm (Photo 1-14)

It is very important that the lead shoulder remains closed until the throwing arm comes forward to open it. This helps keep the weight back and applies more power to the pitch. As the throwing hand comes through, the glove comes toward the body (palm facing the chest) with the elbow next to the left side. This will put the pitcher in better fielding position, ready for any ball hit up the middle. He should remember not to open the lead shoulder too soon, because it will open automatically as the pitching arm moves forward (Photo 1-15).

Stride (Photo 1-16)

The stride should be straight ahead with the toe pointing directly at home plate. This will open the hips and allow the body weight to

Photo 1-16

come forward along with the arm. Be careful of taking too long a stride because it will be difficult for the pitcher to get his weight over a bent front leg. When the stride leg lands, it should be on the ball of the foot with the knee slightly bent rather than on the heel, which will impair the follow-through.

Follow-Through (Photo 1-17)

If the lead leg is bent, the follow-through becomes automatic. If the pitcher lands on the heel of the lead leg, the leg will tend to straighten and he will find it difficult to bend at the waist, making the follow-through incomplete. As he follows through, all the weight is over the lead leg. The arm should snap straight across the chest to the front knee and the back leg comes over parallel to the lead leg putting him in a squared-off position. Remember, a good follow-through is important for speed, control, and a proper fielding position.

The following drills should be used to emphasize the proper techniques as they apply to the developing of sound pitching mechanics.

Photo 1-17

SPECIALIZED PITCHING DRILLS

The Rotation Drill

This drill works on ball rotation and grip. It also focuses on the upper body mechanics, mainly the angle of the arm and lead arm action. The windup, pivot, and stride are eliminated, enabling the pitcher to concentrate on the arm movement, grip, and finger pressure—thus allowing him to see exactly how the ball is moving.

Two pitchers work together at a distance of about 30 feet apart. One pitcher does the drill while the other gets down on a knee and acts like a catcher. *The pitcher throws the ball from half to three-quarter speed and the catcher confirms the type of rotation the ball has.* The catcher looks for backspin on the fast ball, overspin on the curve, or any other movement the pitcher wants.

1. The pitcher sets up with his front leg planted forward as if it were the completion of his regular stride. The hips are slightly open, the lead toe points directly at the target, and the pivot foot is parallel alongside the rubber (Photo 1-18).

Photo 1-18

2. The lead shoulder points at the target in a closed position with the glove higher than the elbow and the back of the glove facing the hitter. The hands are away from the body with the ball well hidden in the webbing of the glove. (This is the position from which the pitcher would normally break his hands.)

3. The pitching arm breaks from the glove and moves down vertically with the wrist hanging loose and the palm of the hand facing down (also known as hand break).

4. The arm then travels like a pendulum—going down, back and up. As this is happening, the lead shoulder remains closed.

5. As the arm reaches the up position, the body weight remains back.

6. As the arm goes forward into the release point, it opens the lead shoulder and transfers the weight forward to the front leg.

7. The pitching elbow is shoulder level or above as the arm comes forward, while the forearm and wrist are perpendicular to the ground. The lead elbow is brought to the side close to the hip with the glove face out.

8. As the ball is released, the pitcher can see its actual rotation—how much spin was applied and the direction it is spinning.

9. After the release, the arm follows through and the weight comes directly over the bent front leg. The arm ends up alongside the stride knee.

This drill is particularly valuable for coaches with no assistants. Since the coach cannot be everywhere at the same time, he can allow the pitchers to help one another.

The Pivot Drill

The key position in the delivery is the pivot. Failure to maintain balance here can impair the arm-body synchronization. The loss of balance makes it difficult to hold the weight back. This, in turn, causes the body to move forward too soon—before the arm. The pitcher usually winds up rushing. The arm either drags behind the body or takes a shortcut to catch up, which will result in short-arming the ball.

Since most problems occur on the pivot, have the pitcher begin in the pivot position while working on the basic mechanics. Once he gets the feel of balance and can put it all together, the windup can easily be added.

1. The pitcher starts in the pivot position with his rear leg parallel to the rubber and slightly flexed (Photo 1-19). He keeps his hands away from the body about chest high at the spot in which he will break them, and brings the lead leg up in a

Photo 1-19

comfortable position with the hip pointed toward the plate. At this point, check to see if the pitcher can hold his balance while his weight is on the rear leg.

2. The pitcher now separates his pitching hand and glove with a vertical swing of the pitching arm, which moves downward with a loose wrist. As the arm swings down, the stride leg remains up and the lead shoulder is closed and pointed toward the batter. The arm then comes up as the stride leg lands preparing the pitcher for the forward acceleration.

3. The forward movement of the arm and body comes next. The stride leg lands on the sole of the foot, rather than the heel, with the knee bent and toe pointed toward the plate. Although the lead leg has landed, the body weight remains back. The arm accelerates forward, opening the lead shoulder and releasing the ball with a full wrist snap. The rear foot pushes off the rubber, aiding the forward acceleration.

4. In the follow-through the arm moves forward to a position alongside the front knee. The pitcher then brings the rear leg up alongside the lead leg placing the body in a square position. The glove hand finishes alongside the hip with the glove open.

Photo 1-20

Pitching from the Set Position (Photo 1-20)

When pitching from the set position, the delivery must be a little quicker than the windup position in order to prevent the runner from getting too big a jump. It is also important to learn to throw to any base from any spot while going into the stretch. Throwing from the hip with a quick dart type of throw will get the ball to the base faster than a full arm sweep. A pitcher must work on quick leg action and fast hands to have a good pickoff move. A quick jump turn is probably the fastest way for a right-hander to get the ball to the base. A left-handed pitcher faces the runner on first base and has more of an advantage to hold him on. He can hang his leg, look at the runner, take a slight forward movement, and still throw to the base. A right-handed pitcher must look over his shoulder to see and check the runner. Once his leg lifts, he must go home with the ball. A good tip for a right-handed pitcher is to hold the ball in the hand when going into the stretch. This will let him throw over to first base from any point as he is going into position. Once the pitcher is ready to release the ball to the batter, the procedure is the same as if he were coming out of the pivot from his regular windup. The only difference is that he may find it necessary to speed up his leg kick, hand break, and release in order to prevent the runner from getting too big a jump.

Taking the Sign from the Stretch Position

The pitcher places his pivot foot (right foot) along the front right-hand side of the rubber in a slightly flexed position. His stride leg is in front, either in a closed (Photo 1-21), open (Photo 1-22), or squared (Photo 1-23) stance. His body is relaxed with the ball in the pitching

Photo 1-21   **Photo 1-22**   **Photo 1-23**

hand alongside his right thigh and his glove by his left thigh. His body is sideways looking toward the catcher for his sign. After receiving his sign, he brings his hands together while checking the runner to a position about belt high. From here, if he decides to deliver the pitch to the batter, he uses the same procedure as if he were pitching from the pivot position in his windup. If he decides to throw to first base, he uses a jump turn or straight body pivot.

Pitching with a Man on Third Base

With runners on third, second and third, or bases loaded, the pitcher may use his regular windup or come to a stretch position. If he uses his stretch position, he comes to a stop, looks at the runner and decides what to do. If he throws to third, he can lift his leg and throw to the third baseman. If he decides to pitch from the windup, he should follow this procedure:

1. Take the sign from the catcher.
2. Look at the runner to keep him honest.
3. Take the windup and throw home.

If the runner breaks towards home plate before the start of his windup, the pitcher should step off the rubber and make the play. The pitcher is now an infielder and the batter cannot swing at the ball.

FILMS TO REVIEW PITCHING FUNDAMENTALS AND MECHANICS

Watching films of his actions can be very helpful to your pitchers. As your pitchers review the films, have them consider the following:

1. Watch your feet first.

   a. Do you overstride or understride? If you land on your heel you are overstriding.
   b. Do you cross over or throw across your body? This habit will tend to make you a bad fielder and a wild pitcher.
   c. After the ball is delivered are you in a fielding position?
   d. When pitching from the stretch, are you lifting your leg high and cradling your body?
   e. Also from the stretch—do you swing your leg around to gain more motion? This will cause you to unload too slowly.

2. Watch your arm and body.

   a. Do you follow through and bend your back after delivering the ball? Never become a straight-up pitcher.

   b. Is your arm moving forward quickly or does it have lazy action?

   c. Do you throw all your pitches from the same position?

   d. Can you call your own pitches from the film?

   e. From the stretch position—does your arm have as quick actions as your legs and body? This is very important.

3. Watch your head.

   a. Do you keep your eyes set on the target or is your head always in motion before throwing the ball?

   b. From the stretch—do you always look at second base one time and then throw? This is a very bad habit to develop because a runner will steal third on you standing up.

   c. Do you vary your head movements to bases? You should. Look short one time and then longer the next. Look one time and then look two or more times.

The good fast-ball pitchers all have quick arms moving forward. If a pitcher is lazy with that arm he can tell it by watching the films. Pitchers can get into slumps, the same as hitters; by the use of films, a pitcher can compare his good games with his bad ones. This way he can notice and correct his mistakes in a short period of time.

BUILDING YOUR PITCHING PROGRAM:
Drills, Warm-ups, and Training Objectives

2

Once you have taught your players the basics of pitching (as covered in Chapter 1), you'll be ready to start building a pitching program geared to your own team's strengths and needs. This chapter covers the main parts of any careful pitching program:

1. Drills—the heart of any team's training. You'll find ten of the most common pitching situations and how to deal with them, drills for fielding balls and for covering baserunners, combination drills for the pitcher and the rest of the infield to practice, and a special indoor drill covering bunt reaction.
2. Warm-up procedures—how to develop consistency, the importance of long and short relievers, and overall conditioning tips for both on and off the field.
3. Training objectives—featuring a weight training plan that promotes muscular strength, endurance, flexibility, and speed.

A sample pitching chart and scouting report are also included to help you in setting up your game plans.

TEN FUNDAMENTAL FIELDING SITUATIONS AND HOW TO REACT TO THEM

A pitcher must be skilled not only in delivering the pitch but in fielding the ball as well. We have discovered these responses are the most effective in the following fielding situations every pitcher must face. Drill your pitchers until these become automatic.

1. *Fielding bunts and topped rollers*—use skip step when possible.

   - No runners on base—throw to first base.
   - Runner on first base—force at second base if possible.
   - Runners on first and second base—force at third base.
   - Runner on second base only—tag play at third base.

2. *The Comeback Ball*—use skip step.

   - No runners on base—wait for first baseman to get to the base and then throw hard.
   - Runner on first base—throw to second baseman or shortstop covering second base.
   - Runners on first and second base—use 1-6-3 or 1-4-3 double play.
   - Bases loaded—home plate to first base.

3. *Backing up bases*—get off mound quickly.

   - Stand 35–40 feet behind the base if possible.
   - Make sure to block the ball.
   - Go the short way off the mound.
   - If in doubt, go halfway between bases and see how the play develops.
   - With no one on base and the batter singles—keep an eye on the ball in case of a deflected throw.

4. *Covering first base*—break off the mound hard on all balls hit to your left. Stay on inside of the foul line and touch inside of base with the right foot.

5. *Covering second base*—when the shortstop and second baseman both go after a short fly in centerfield, break hard to second.

6. *Covering third base*—when there's a fly ball down the left field line and both third baseman and shortstop go for it, move to third.

7. *Covering home plate*—on all wild pitches and passed balls with runners on base—if the catcher is having difficulty locating the ball, run in, pointing at the ball and telling him where it is (visual and verbal signs). Also cover on all foul flies that the catcher goes for with runners on base.

8. *Covering comeback plays*—charge all runners that are hung up on comeback balls, run them back to the last base and throw to the infielder, continuing into a backup position.

9. *Runner on first base breaks prematurely while the pitcher is in set position*—the pitcher should step back off the pitching rubber with the pivot foot.

10. *Runners on first and third base*—when the runner on first base breaks prematurely, the pitcher should step back off the pitching rubber, turn by way of third base to check and hold the runner, and then throw to the second baseman in a "cheating" position.

PRECISION DRILLS FOR PITCHERS

Fielding Bunts and Topped Rollers

In the first half of the drill (no runner on) the pitcher throws with a full windup, then changes to the stretch for the last half of the drill (runner on first base). The *first baseman* plays the deep position while the pitcher throws with the full windup and holds the runner on base when the stretch position is used. The *second baseman* plays his normal position until the stretch position is used, then he shortens up and shades slightly toward second base. The *third baseman* plays his normal position until the stretch position is used; then he plays one or two steps on the infield grass. The *catcher* is in his regular receiving position behind home plate.

With no runner on base

The pitcher delivers using a full windup. After receiving the pitch, the catcher tosses a bunt or simulated roller in front of the plate. Easy ones should be tossed to start; then, when the pitcher is warmer, more difficult ones can be thrown down the foul lines. The pitcher *must* hustle off the mound and get to the ball as quickly as possible with his body in control, field it in front with two hands, take an aggressive step toward first base and throw hard to the first baseman, aiming at his face. The second baseman backs up the first baseman, the shortstop covers second base, the third baseman covers third base, the catcher calls the play loud and clear and points to where the ball is to be thrown, then covers home plate. (See Illustration 2-1.)

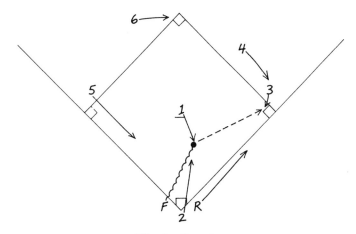

Illustration 2-1

With runner on first base

The pitcher delivers using the stretch position. The catcher again tosses a simulated bunt. The pitcher goes through the same procedure, throwing to either the first or second baseman, whoever is covering. The pitcher concentrates on keeping his throws on the inside of the base, thus avoiding hitting the runner. Throwing over the runner makes it difficult for the first or second baseman to see the throw.

The first baseman charges if he has a play, or backs up to take the throw if he does not. The second baseman waits until the bunt is down and then breaks to cover first base. If the first baseman has backed up to take the throw, the second baseman backs up the first baseman. The shortstop waits until the bunt is down, then covers second base. The third baseman charges with body in control and hands ready as the pitcher delivers. If the pitcher fields the ball, the third baseman retreats and covers third base. The catcher repeats the previous routine and calls the play, "first" or "second" in this case. If the third baseman fields the ball, the catcher continues on to cover third base.

The second or first baseman, whoever covers, *must* give a good inside target facing the throw, left foot on the inside corner of the base, hands out in front of the body and ready for the throw.

Although the drill is designed primarily for the pitchers, the catcher may toss a bunt to the first baseman, third baseman, or himself, to simulate those game situations. (See Illustration 2-2.)

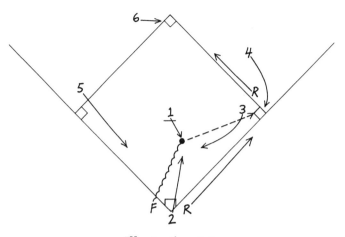

Illustration 2-2

With runners on first and second

The *pitcher* throws from the stretch position. The *catcher* is in his normal receiving position behind the plate. The *first baseman* plays from two to three steps in on the grass and charges with body in control as the pitcher delivers. He is responsible for any bunt from the first base line to the pitcher's mound. The *second baseman* shortens up and shades toward first base; when the bunt is down he covers first base. The *shortstop* shortens up slightly, perhaps three or four steps behind and just off the right shoulder of the runner. It is his intention to allow the runner a fairly large lead if he will take it; when the bunt is down he covers second base. The *third baseman* plays one step in on the grass and advances one more step as the pitcher delivers. He then holds to see how the play develops.

The pitcher delivers and after his follow-through breaks to a spot on the third base line about one third of the way from home to third base (30 feet). He has his body in control and is responsible for all bunts from the third base line to the pitchers mound. He does not wait for the ball to be bunted, but breaks immediately to the spot described after delivering the pitch. The first baseman is responsible for balls bunted behind the charging pitcher. The pitcher gets to the bunt as quickly as possible, fields the ball with two hands out in front, and whirls to his glove-hand side. With a strong forearm flip he throws to the third baseman, who, seeing that the pitcher will field the ball, has retreated to third base to take the throw. If possible, the third baseman stretches out like a first baseman to complete the play more quickly.

In making his throw after fielding the bunt, the pitcher must concentrate on whirling and throwing in one motion to avoid losing time. If he straightens up and draws his arm way back, he will lose precious time to the runner who is in full stride. He should aim his quick, forearm flip at the third baseman's face, where it will be easy to handle on a stretch.

The third baseman fields any sharply bunted ball that gets by the pitcher and fires to second or first as directed by the catcher, who once again calls the play. The first baseman fields all the bunts in his area and with a skip step fires to third, if that is the call, or to second or first. He must be aggressive and expect to make the play on the lead runner at third base. The catcher breaks out to field any short bunt immediately in front of the plate and fires to third, if possible, or to another base if that is appropriate. If not fielding the bunt, he calls the play for the pitcher, third baseman, or first baseman.

We have purposely delayed outlining the most important part of this drill, and furthermore, have taken it out of its natural sequence, to impress that if this particular technique is not mastered, your players will have a very rough time getting the lead runner. If you will recall, the shortstop plays just off the right shoulder of the runner at second base and fairly deep, perhaps four steps back, encouraging him to take a large lead. The pitcher comes to his set or to his stretch position and looks back at second base. Simultaneously, the shortstop breaks behind the runner toward second base. The runner, losing sight of the shortstop over his right shoulder, and possibly hearing a warning

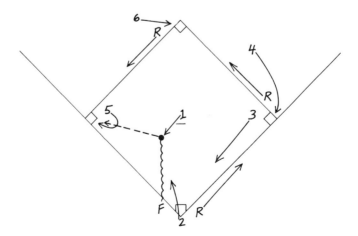

Illustration 2-3

from his third base coach, is forced to break back to second base himself. Even with a smaller lead he will shift his body weight from his front to his rear foot nearest second base. When he sees this happen, the pitcher immediately delivers to the plate. Thus we have the ball bunted when the lead runner is moving, or at the very least leaning, in the wrong direction. If all the fielders do their jobs properly, you have a good chance of cutting down the lead man and breaking up that big inning. (See Illustration 2-3.)

Runner on second only with bunt in order

If there is a runner on second base only, all the techniques are exactly the same with the exception of those carried out by the third baseman. Before the play begins, we remind our players that in case of a bunt, the third baseman retreats to third base, straddles the bag, receives the throw and tags the runner sliding in.

The catcher, in calling the play, realizes the pitcher has less time before making the throw to third. The pitcher should aim knee high to help make the tag quicker and easier. If the third baseman judges that the pitcher will not be able to field the bunt, he charges, fields the bunt, and throws the batter out at first base. (See Illustration 2-4.)

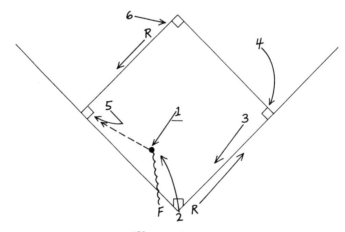

Illustration 2-4

Comeback Ball

With runner on first or first and second

The infield is set at double-play depth. The *pitcher* works from the stretch position. The pitcher checks the position of the shortstop, as he would during the game, since they will work together in the event of a comeback ball.

Using the stretch position, the pitcher delivers to the plate. The coach, standing close to the plate with a fungo bat and extra ball, hits a comebacker to the pitcher. The pitcher fields the ball out in front with two hands, if possible, whirls to his glove-hand side, takes an aggressive skip step toward second base, and fires hard and face high to the shortstop, who by this time is in motion toward second base. The pitcher's job is to lead the shortstop who is breaking toward second base. The shortstop then proceeds to catch the ball, touch second base, and throw on to first base to complete the double play. In a case where the shortstop is slow in getting into motion, or has a long way to go, the pitcher may take an extra skip step to time the play and to keep himself in motion toward his target, thus cutting down on the possibility of a wild throw or injury.

On the play, the second baseman backs up the shortstop at second base, the first baseman covers first base, the third baseman covers third base, and the catcher covers home plate. With a runner on first base only, there is only one change: The first baseman would hold the runner on, rather than play behind him at double-play depth.

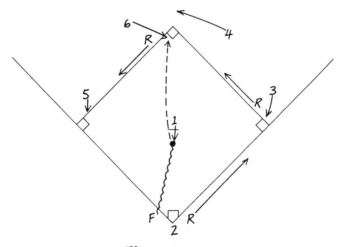

Illustration 2-5

You will also find it profitable to spend a few minutes on the same play with the second baseman as the pivot man. If a strong right-handed pull hitter should be at the plate, your shortstop would be fairly deep and toward the third base hole, while your second baseman would be only a few steps from second base. In this case, as the pitcher whirls to his glove-hand side and takes the skip step, the second baseman will have already reached the bag. The pitcher, therefore, should throw at the second baseman's face just over the first base side of the bag. The catcher, as always, points and calls the play. (See Illustration 2-5.)

With bases loaded

With the bases loaded and less than two out, the catcher reminds the pitcher to go home with the comebacker. The pitcher practices his short windup (or set position) with a runner on third base and delivers to the plate. The *catcher* is in his normal receiving position behind the plate. The *shortstop and second baseman* are at double-play depth. The *first and third basemen* play opposite their respective bases and judge the distance from the foul line according to the hitter. The second baseman and the shortstop look for the double play around the horn, if possible, or the force at home, depending on the type of ground ball. The third baseman and the first baseman look for the force at the plate and possible double play at first base on the hitter, on all ground balls hit directly at them, to the foul-line side, or half-speed that they must charge. On hard ground balls to the second base side they try for the double play via second base and back to first.

The coach hits a comebacker to the pitcher, who fields the ball out in front with two hands. He then takes a skip step toward home plate, and makes a quick, dart throw to the catcher at home plate. The pitcher should have in mind accuracy, not power. If he throws the ball too hard, he will handcuff the catcher and cut down the possibilities of a double play.

When the ball is hit to the pitcher, the catcher comes up and plants his right foot on the plate with his hands high and ready. He catches the throw, if accurate, while moving out, with a skip step into the diamond and up toward first base. This should be done aggressively, to clear himself from the runner attempting to score from third base and at the same time taking himself well inside the runner going to first base. Now he has an easy throw to the first baseman, who should be giving that good inside target.

The third baseman covers third base, the second baseman and shortstop cover second base and back up second base, the first baseman covers first base. Once in a while, make your catcher go through these drills with his gear on so he gets used to making the plays under game conditions. (See Illustration 2-6.)

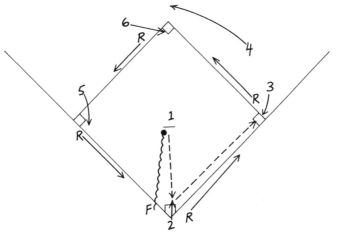

Illustration 2-6

Pitcher Covering First Base

Whenever a left-handed hitter comes to the plate, or a right-handed hitter who is a late swinger is at bat, the catcher *always* reminds the pitcher to get off the mound fast and cover first base in the event of a ground ball to the right side.

With no runners on base

The *pitcher* takes his full windup, the *catcher* is in his normal receiving position behind the plate, and the infield is playing deep. The coach, once again, is next to the plate with a fungo and extra ball.

When the pitcher delivers to the catcher, the coach hits a ground ball to the first baseman. When the ball is hit, and not before, the pitcher breaks hard but with body in control to a spot on the first base line. He turns and runs parallel with the line toward first base with his hands high and ready. (See Photo 2-1.) The pitcher must be sure to run up the inside of the first base line to avoid interference with the runner, who must run outside the foul line for the last 45 feet to first base.

The first baseman who has fielded the ball must now feed the moving pitcher quickly and accurately. On all balls hit at him or to the foul line side, he will be able to take several steps toward first base and lob a soft underhand toss to the pitcher coming up the inside of the line. He should take the ball out of his glove and *show* it to the

Photo 2-1

Photo 2-2

pitcher as he prepares to make his underhand toss. He should aim his toss chest high and to the inside of the base. In addition, he should try to get the ball to the pitcher a few steps before he reaches first base so that he can glance down and make sure he touches the base.

The pitcher receives the throw, touches the inside corner of the base and bounces off aggressively into the infield (Photo 2-2). This action avoids any contact or chance of injury to himself or the runner. When the pitcher is coming off the bag into the infield, make him keep his hands high, whirl to his glove side, face the infield and cock his arm ready to throw. This part of the drill prepares the pitcher to make the next play when another runner may be trying to advance. You must insist on second effort and mental alertness!

On a ball hit deep to the second base side of the first baseman, or on a ball that is fumbled by the first baseman, the pitcher (if he has time) should stretch out like a first baseman to complete the play more quickly (Illustration 2-7).

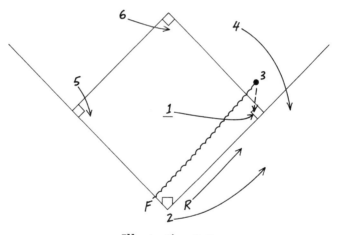

Illustration 2-7

With a runner on first base

The *pitcher* will use his stretch position and the catcher will be in his normal receiving position behind the plate. The infield will be set at double-play depth and the first baseman will be holding the runner on.

When the pitcher delivers to the catcher, the coach hits a ground ball wide to the second base side of first base. The first baseman, who has broken off the bag on the pitch, continues to his right and fields the ball. He throws to the shortstop at second base who has "rounded" into second base on the inside corner. Since the first baseman was holding the runner on, he will field the ball on the grass and this throw to the inside avoids any trouble with the runner going from first to second.

The pitcher breaks over as quickly as possible to cover first base. The first baseman going well to his right cannot come back in time. The pitcher straddles first base, facing toward second base this time, and receives the return throw from the shortstop. He tries to stretch out like a first baseman to complete the play more quickly.

Sometimes your pitchers will start to "anticipate" in that they will break toward first base before the coach hits the ball. A quick cure is a bunt down the third base line rather than a ground ball to the right side. The pitcher looks bad breaking to first base when he should be fielding a bunt. The lesson stays with him and he usually gets some good-natured reminders from his fellow pitchers! (See Illustration 2-8.)

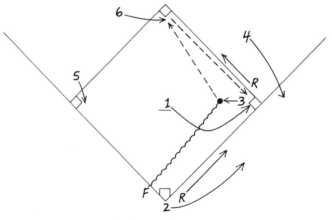

Illustration 2-8

All-Purpose Pitching Drill

In this drill, the team can go through all the pitching drills in a short period of time. Line up three catchers, one behind home plate, and one each on the first and third base sides. You should have your pitchers in three lines at the pitcher's mound. One line should be right on the rubber and the other two lines off toward the first and third base lines.

A first baseman is placed in the deep fielding position behind first base. The middle infielders are placed at shortstop and one middle infielder is placed between second base and first base. The third baseman is placed at third base in a bunt situation.

The drill begins with the catcher on the first base side throwing a ground ball to the first baseman, who fields the ball and tosses it to the pitcher covering first base. The pitcher covering first base is on the line nearest first base.

The catcher, who is directly behind home plate, throws a ground ball to the pitcher who is on the rubber. The pitcher fields the ball, turns, and throws to the middle infielder who is covering second base. The middle infielder catches the ball, makes his pivot and throws the ball to the middle infielder who is standing halfway between first and second base. The catcher on the third-base side rolls a bunt down the third base line and the pitcher on the line nearest third base breaks toward the line, fields the bunt, and throws to the third baseman covering the base. (See Illustration 2-9.)

All three drills proceed simultaneously. The pitchers should alternate lines so that they go through all phases of the pitching drills.

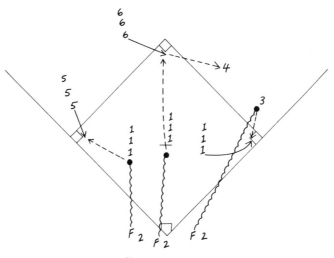

Illustration 2-9

Indoor Bunt Reaction Drill for Pitchers

Four bases are set up in the gym and a player is placed at each base. The pitcher goes in the middle and faces one of the bases. He faces home so that the base to his left is first; to his right is third and behind him is second.

The pitcher takes his stretch and throws home. The player catching the ball rolls it on the ground and calls out a base. The pitcher fields the ball and throws to the base called. The base that was just thrown to now becomes the new home plate and the next base to the pitcher's left becomes first; to his right becomes third and behind him becomes second.

The pitcher goes into his stretch, delivers home and reacts to the bunted ball and the base called for. To whichever base the ball is thrown from the bunt becomes the next home plate.

This drill allows the pitcher to work on his fielding and throwing in bunt situations. It is also used for conditioning.

Curve Ball Drill for Pitchers

This drill is designed to teach the pitcher the proper grip and rotation of the curve ball.

A black line is drawn in the middle of a baseball in the same direction the seams are running. Two pitchers stand about 30 feet apart and throw the ball to one another. Each pitcher grips the ball with the middle finger and thumb running along the seams. One pitcher throws the ball while the receiving pitcher looks for the proper rotation and break. The four seams and the black line should have overspin. If the spin is to the side, the receiver reminds the pitcher to get his fingers on top of the ball rather than to the side.

The marked ball can also be used in the rotation drill described previously.

First and Third Bunt Situation Drill

Two pitchers are placed in the middle of the gym floor facing two catchers at home plate. The catchers are about ten feet alongside one another in a crouch position. The pitchers stand about ten feet alongside one another in their stretch position facing the catchers. A fielder is on first and another on third. The pitcher delivers the ball to the catcher he is throwing to and the ball is rolled out toward third and first. The pitcher on the right fields and throws to third and the pitcher on the left throws to first. When the play is completed, the pitchers come back to the middle and change places. The pitcher who has just practiced throwing to first now throws to third and the pitcher who threw to third now throws to first.

WARM-UP PROCEDURES FOR PITCHING CONSISTENCY

Here are some helpful tips for both your starting and relieving pitchers.

Tips for the Starter

- Throw from a pitcher's mound if available.
- Throw at the same angle and direction as the mound on the field.
- Vary the length of warm-up depending on
  Temperature and wind conditions
  Type of musculature
  Past experience
- Always do some jogging, stretching, and loosening-up exercises before starting to throw.
- Spend at least half of the warm-up time throwing at medium to three-quarter speed, concentrating on control.
- Use all pitches during the warm-up—fast ball, curve, change-up, etc.
- Make sure some throwing is done from the set position.
- Remember that it is better to warm up too much than too little. The dangerous parts of the game for the pitcher are innings one and two, and eight and nine. Like piloting a plane, the two most dangerous parts of the flight are the takeoff and the landing.
- Always warm up throwing to spots—inside, outside, high and low in the strike zone.
- Throw the last 15 pitches of the warm-up in the bullpen at game velocity.
- Keep the first few warm-up pitches on the game mound at medium speed until the footing for the stride is established.

You should designate the long and short relievers before the game and they should be in the bullpen, not the dugout. Set up the relief men with the best man for the end of the game.

Tips for the Reliever

- Pay attention—know the score, the number of outs, and the game situation.

- Hurry—don't hesitate—when told to warm up.
- If needed in a hurry, play catch quickly at a short distance and continue the regular routine.
- Have someone in the bullpen keep the pitcher informed about developments—the pitcher and catcher should not stop and look at the game between pitches.
- Be ready even if never called on to pitch during a game. Keep tossing at medium speed and concentrating on control until directed otherwise.
- Run to the mound when called into the game, get familiar with the mound, and take warm-ups from the stretch or windup depending on the game situation.
- Be ready with your best pitch.

GENERAL CONDITIONING WORKOUTS

On the Field

Running poles. Pitchers run from foul pole to foul pole several times. This is a good warming up exercise that helps build up endurance.

Pivot and rotation drills. Both of these drills work at loosening up players and developing skills. (See Chapter 1 for how to set up the drills.)

Pickups. The coach and pitcher should stand 15 feet apart and facing each other. The coach rolls the ball to the pitcher's right. The pitcher shuffles to his right, keeping his body low and staying in good fielding position. After fielding the ball, the pitcher returns the ball to the coach with an underhand toss. The coach then rolls the ball to the pitcher's left. This should be repeated for 20 to 25 repetitions. As the players get into better condition, the repetitions should be increased to 50. The pitcher should always use his glove during the drill. This drill helps develop leg and back muscles.

Double-ball drill. This has the same principle as the pickup drill, except that the coach uses two baseballs. The second ball is tossed as the pitcher fields the first ball. The purpose is to provide a quicker pace to the pickup drill.

Pepper drill. This works on hand and eye coordination while developing quick hands and feet. It also helps the pitcher learn to field his position. The drill is done with a batter and a few fielders standing about 30 feet from one another. The fielders throw a ball and the batter hits it back at them on the ground. The fielders work on their fielding skills.

Wind sprints. These develop the body and strengthen the legs by running short distances with bursts of speed, for example, running as fast as possible toward a base or a ball.

Calisthenics and stretching. Every coach will have his own favorite exercises he will want his team to practice. Emphasize the importance of proper loosening up before playing to stretch the muscles and help prevent injuries.

Off the Field

Equally important to all responsible players is not only their training on the field, but also their training off the field. Good diet and nutritional habits are a must for players who want to stay healthy. Tell your players to get enough sleep (eight hours is the general rule of thumb). Smoking and drinking are two obvious habits to avoid.

Sacrifice and discipline must be exercised by the players *themselves*. Tell your players that they must "pay the price" and refrain from the partying scene—the reward will be athletes at their maximum playing ability!

CONDITIONING TO PITCH

Throwing

- Always throw at a target. Maintain control—even when just playing catch.
- Throwing helps to strengthen the arm. Muscles must be used to be developed. Remember always to *throw with a purpose*.

Batting practice

- Maintain control—try to make every pitch a strike.
- Control of entire repertoire—you should be able to throw breaking pitches and changes on request.
- Alternate with windup and stretch.

- Practice holding men on base.
- Never throw at batting practice while wearing a windbreaker.

Fielding drills (mound drills)

Dummy scrimmage—coach fungoes ball, base runners are used to set up game situations.

Intrasquad games

WEIGHT TRAINING

Strength is important to the pitcher, and indeed to all baseball players, because it

- Helps protect against injury
- Increases muscular endurance, thus enabling the player to compete for a longer duration without fatigue
- Lengthens the playing lifetime of a player

Objective of the Strength-Training Program

An effective weight/strength-training program will strive to increase

- muscular strength
- muscular endurance
- joint flexibility, and
- muscular speed

With these objectives in mind, your players should observe the following fundamentals when participating in a strength-training program:

Do all repetitions throughout with a complete *range of motion*. Full range of motion refers to when a muscle is fully contracted and extended during the exercise in which you are working that particular muscle.

Do all repetitions slowly, making sure to pause briefly at the fully contracted position and at the starting position.

If a player can do twelve or more repetitions, then the weight is too light and 5 to 10 pounds should be added. If he cannot lift the weight six times, the weight is too heavy.

Do repetitions in a smooth and controlled manner. Avoid jerking of the weights.

Do all repetitions with each player competing against himself, not other players.

A stretching program should be done before and after weight training.

Strength-training programs should not replace other phases of your program, nor should they be the main ingredient. It is important that your players continue their running, throwing, and hitting. However, when done properly, the strength-training program can be a highly beneficial and rewarding addition to the development of your team.

This program is designed to fit the needs of most athletes. Use the Universal machine or free weights to do the following exercises. The body areas that benefit from these exercises are listed in parenthesis. We have listed the suggested order for performing the exercises, in order to work from the weaker to stronger muscles.

1. Bench press (chest)
2. Curls (arms)
3. Triceps extension (arms)
4. Military press (shoulders)
5. Lat pulls (back)
6. Dips (arms and chest)
7. Sit-ups (stomach)
8. Step-ups on bench (legs)

Hanging between sets will keep muscles extended.

Remember, strength training should never be done alone, and you, as the coach, should supervise all activities.

THE PITCHING CHART

Each team should keep a pitching chart for the following reasons:

- It gives a count of the number of pitches thrown in the game for each pitcher.
- It allows the pitcher to see what pitch was hit by each batter.
- It shows the pitching pattern of the opposing pitchers to each batter.
- It allows each pitcher to analyze his game after it is completed in order to improve himself.

The chart should be simple and easy to understand. A sample chart is shown on page 43.

How to Use the Chart

Tape together a blue and red pen in order to get the use of both colors.

Use a number system for each pitch thrown to each batter. For example, if six pitches are thrown to the batter, there should be six numbers (1–6), with "1" meaning the first pitch thrown and "6" meaning the last.

All red numbers indicate fast balls.

All blue numbers indicate curve balls.

A red number with a line underneath means a change.

A blue number with a line underneath means a slider.

All foul balls have a line through the number (5).

When the ball is hit, the number is circled and should have an extended line indicating what occurred: ⑤ —————6-4.

At the end of each inning the number of pitches is recorded at the bottom and a running count is used for all innings that follow. For example:

Inning	10	15	15	18	10	15	10	10	10
Total	10	25	40	58	68	83	93	103	113

Chart all strikes in the upper or lower half of the strike zone.

1
2

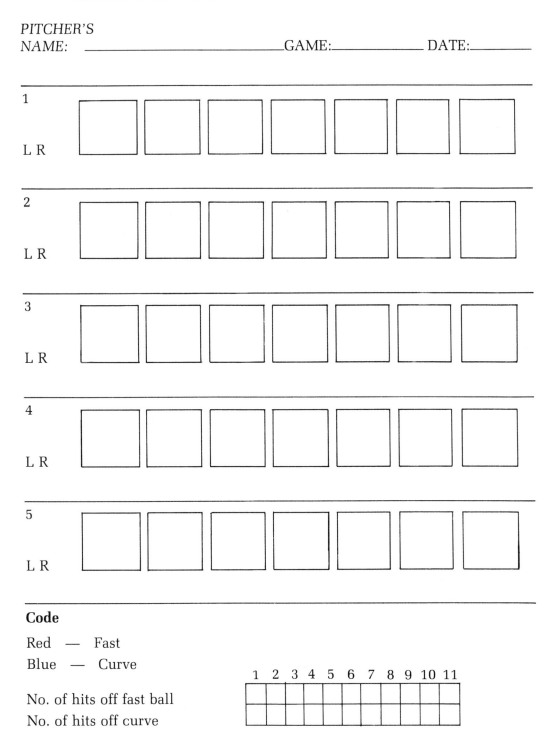

PITCHER'S
NAME: _____ GAME:_____ DATE:_____

1

L R

2

L R

3

L R

4

L R

5

L R

Code

Red — Fast
Blue — Curve

No. of hits off fast ball
No. of hits off curve

1	2	3	4	5	6	7	8	9	10	11

SCOUTING REPORT

Have your pitchers study opposing team scouting reports carefully. When you have people prepare these reports, ask them to:

- List batting orders of each team by player number, right or left-handed batter, and defensive position. For example: 1 - #24 - bats right, throws right, 6 (SS). Include: at bats, hits, walks, strikeouts, RBI, runs scored and SBs.

- List individual offensive and defensive strengths and weaknesses of each player on both teams. For example: #24 hits fast ball well, has trouble with curve; defensively—strong arm, average range, weak on DP pivot. Also include base-running and bunting ability.

  Pitchers should be carefully studied for strengths and weaknesses, idiosyncrasies, tendencies, pickoff move, fielding ability, etc.

- List *team* offensive and defensive strengths and weaknesses, and tendencies. Include strategies. For example: executes cutoffs and relays well, cannot take the extra base; had trouble handling the first and third double steal situation—threw back to the pitcher every time in this situation and allowed runner to reach second uncontested.

  Offensively, the team bunted early in game (sacrifice), and played for one run from the first inning on. The team does not run much, but prefers to bunt men into scoring position. Did not attempt to hit and run.

A sample scouting sheet is shown on pages 45 and 46. You, of course, can change the Sample Scouting Report to suit your own needs.

Team characteristics

Include in this section *cutoffs and relays*, defensing and *bunt* (good or bad, and how), handling the first and third situation (how, and how well), making the DP. Offensively, include: Baserunning (overall team speed and ability, aggressiveness, etc.), execution of the bunt (sacrifice, squeeze), hit and run (do they or don't they, and how well), first and third situation.

Additional comments

Include in this section whatever you think may be of use to your team. For example, you believe that you've discovered their signals system—the key is the right hand to the belt, etc.

	THROWS	FAST BALL	BREAKING PITCH	OTHER PITCHES	ARM ANGLE	STRETCH POSITION	ADDITIONAL COMMENTS
NAME							
ARMSTRONG	R	GOOD VELOCITY NO MOVEMENT	USES SLIDER NO CURVE	SHOWED ONE CHANGE UP	3/4	AVERAGE 1/4 TO PLATE	POWER PITCHER. WORKS FAST. FAIR SLIDER CAN BUNT ON HIM.
BARTEK	L	AVERAGE SINKER BALL PITCHER	GOOD CURVE FAIR SLIDER	SHOWED NONE	3/4	GOOD. GOOD MOVE TO FIRST	CUTIE, CHANGES SPEEDS. WILL NOT OVERPOWER YOU.

PITCHER'S SCOUTING REPORT

TEAM ___TITANS___ VS. ___SUNS___

Sample Pitcher's Scouting Report

SCOUTING REPORT

TEAM __TITANS__ VS. __SUNS__

NAME	POS	BATS	THROWS	FIELDING	RUNNING	HITTING	STRENGTHS AND WEAKNESS	ADDITIONAL COMMENTS
JONES	CF	L	L	GOOD BEST OF OUTFIELDERS	GOOD SPEED	SPRAY HITTER NO POWER	DO NOT LET ON BASE. WILL RUN. FAIR ARM.	CAN'T HIT BREAKING PITCH, ALSO JAM HIM.
SMITH	2B	R	R	QUICK HANDS GOOD PIVOT	FAIR	SPRAY HITTER LIKES TO BUNT	NO POWER	LIKES TO HIT TO RIGHT FIELD. KEEP BALL INSIDE.
WILLIAMS	1B	L	L	AVERAGE	SLOW	GOOD POWER PULL HITTER	DOES NOT RUN WELL	PITCH HIM LOW AND AWAY. MIX UP SPEED.
ALBERT	RF	L	L	AVERAGE WEAK ARM	AVERAGE	BEST POWER ON TEAM	TOUGH OUT	HAS TROUBLE WITH OFF-SPEED PITCHES.
O'NEIL	SS	R	R	GOOD GOES WELL TO LEFT	GOOD AGGRESSIVE ON BASES	HITS TO ALL FIELDS	BEST ARM ON TEAM	PITCH INSIDE WITH HARD STUFF.
DOE	LF	L	L	POOR BAD JUMP ON BALL	AVERAGE	FAIR POWER LUNGES AT BALL	POOR ARM GOOD FAST BALL HITTER	OFF-SPEED PITCHES GIVE HIM TROUBLE.
PHILIPS	3B	R	R	AVERAGE GOOD ARM	GOOD	GOOD POWER CAN BE FOOLED EASILY	SWINGS AT BAD PITCHES	MAKE HIM CHASE BAD PITCHES WHEN PITCHER IS AHEAD IN COUNT.
NOLAN	C	R	R	GOOD HANDS GOOD ARM	SLOW NO THREAT	WEAK — SLOW BAT	CALLS A GOOD GAME BEHIND PLATE	SLOW BAT FEED HIM FAST BALLS.
WILSON	DH	L	L	—	GOOD SPEED	SPRAY HITTER	GOOD BUNTER VERY FAST	WILL STEAL BASES WHEN ON. MAKE HIM HIT BALL IN AIR.

GENERAL COMMENTS ON FIELD
1. FIELD IS SHORT TO LEFT - 310 FEET
2. FAST INFIELD
3. BACKSTOP IN CLOSE
4. HIGH MOUND
5. RIGHT FIELD SUN FIELD
6. POWER ALLEYS - 375 FEET

Sample Scouting Report

CATCHING:
Skills for Perfection

3

"We need the big guy behind the plate!" How often do you hear this, and how often is this statement misunderstood by young and old coaches alike? Just what does "big guy" mean? physically big? mentally big? Catching is the second most demanding position on the field, and yes, it would help to have a big, physical person behind the plate, but not one who is just big and lacking in many other necessary qualifications. We have come a long way from the mentality of placing just a big, slow player behind the plate, because experience has shown that the catcher's position requires some very important qualifications and abilities.

WHAT SHOULD YOU LOOK FOR IN A CATCHER?

1. *Leadership potential:* Every team needs a leader on the field—a man who takes charge and quarterbacks the team. You want your catcher to be that man. Your catcher should become "The Take Charge Individual," "The Director on the Field." We have all used these titles in the past, and rightly so. The catcher sees everything in front of him. He directs, keeps his teammates on their toes, and calls the game for his pitcher.

2. *Physical strength:* Look for an individual who is rugged and durable. He must be ready for contact, and be willing to use his body to block pitches in the dirt.

3. *Quickness and agility:* How often have you seen a game won or lost because of a catcher's failure to shift his weight quickly in blocking or catching a poorly thrown ball? Your catcher must be agile in shifting for pitches, fielding bunts, and catching pop-ups.

4. *Good throwing arm:* A strong throwing arm and a quick release are essential. The catcher can compensate for having a

"good" arm and not a "great" arm if the receiver has a quick release. Getting rid of the ball quickly is often the difference between a safe or out call.

If you find an individual who possesses these qualifications, then the task of teaching him certain fundamentals may become easier for him to master.

FUNDAMENTAL CATCHING SKILLS

As any other position, catching requires certain fundamental skills that must be "perfected" if your catcher wants to be effective.

Stance

There are two basic stances a catcher must have. One is when he is giving his signs, and the other when he is in position to receive the pitch. Many coaches feel that a catcher can be in a different position with no one on base because he doesn't have to worry about throwing out any baserunners. You want your catcher to be in the same position whether or not there are men on base. This keeps him ready for bunts or any slow rollers out in front of the plate, and enables him to jump out quickly, ready for the play.

Stance when giving signs (Photo 3-1)

The first thing a catcher must be concerned with is to make sure that any member of the opposing team does not see his sign. When he goes into his stance this fact must be taken into consideration.

The catcher assumes his stance by squatting down and putting his weight on the balls of his feet. His left wrist rests on his left knee with the back of his glove facing the third base line. This is to prevent the third base coach from seeing his sign. The right knee points toward the pitcher. The right hand, palm in, is placed on the inside of the thigh just to the right of the crotch. This prevents the first base coach from seeing the sign. After the sign is given, the catcher goes into his stance for receiving the pitch.

Stance when receiving the pitch (Photo 3-2)

The first thing the catcher must do is get as close to the batter as he can without interfering with his swing. He should be able to almost touch the batter's back elbow with his glove. The catcher must

Photo 3-1   **Photo 3-2**

get into a position where he can receive the ball and get out as quickly as possible. His feet are slightly more than shoulder width apart with the toe of his right foot on line with the ball of his left foot. He should be on the balls of his feet. The important thing to remember is to make sure he has good balance so he can move quickly. The stance should be comfortable, not allowing his tail to be too high, nor his shoulders too forward; an awkward stance can create a pelvic strain. If his tail is too low, it restricts lateral movement. The arms should be relaxed and away from the body with arms and elbows outside the knees.

When giving the target make sure the glove is where he wants the ball, and keep his hand relaxed. The bare hand is kept just behind the thumb part of the catcher's glove with the thumb touching the index finger in a relaxed manner. If a catcher uses a hinged glove, he can keep his hand behind his back when there are no runners on base.

Receiving and Throwing (Photo 3-3)

When getting ready to receive the pitch, the catcher gets as close to the batter as he can. He should be in his stance giving a good target. He must be aware that he wants the umpire to get a good look at every pitch thrown. A good receiver is smooth and fluid, making as few motions as possible. When he receives the ball, the catcher gives slightly with his hands as he catches the ball.

Photo 3-3

The toughest part is catching the pitch in the dirt. When the pitch is in the dirt, he drops to his knees with his glove in the middle. When he goes down on both knees, the shin guards are out of the way and the soft part of his body is in good position to block the ball. He keeps his mask and chin in tight to his body and looks at the ball all the way. His shoulders and body are square so that if the ball hits him, it will bounce out in front of him. When receiving a pitch from the knees up, he catches the ball with the fingers up and the heel of the glove down. If the pitch is lower, he catches the ball with the fingers down and the heel of the glove up.

When throwing the ball to a base, the catcher's body should be balanced, unless it is a bunt or slow roller that requires a quick throw to get the runner. He uses an overhand delivery gripping the ball across the four seams. The release must be a quick, short, snappy type. The throw is made from the shoulder and is not a complete sweep of the arm.

To throw, the catcher shifts his weight to his back foot and rotates his shoulders to the right while he brings the ball back over the right shoulder. He keeps his eyes on the target, cocks his arm just back of the ear, and completes his throw as quickly as he can. The ball is released with a vigorous wrist and arm snap while pushing off his right foot onto his left foot. The catcher's footwork, the manner in which he shifts his body into the throw, will determine his effectiveness. By shifting his body correctly, he will have the rhythm, power, and quickness to get rid of the ball in a hurry.

Shifting the body

A good example of proper shifting of the body is seen in a catcher's ability to step correctly and throw when catching either an inside or outside pitch. This can be easily seen by referring to the catcher's right or bare hand. When a ball is to his bare hand or right side, the catcher steps with his right foot first. On pitches to his glove or left side, the catcher steps with his left foot first. This should be practiced until it becomes automatic.

The catcher must get squarely in front of the pitch. He should go into the ball and not catch the ball flat-footed; his weight must be slightly forward.

Framing

One of the most important skills for a catcher to master is that of *framing*. Proper framing can increase the umpire's strike zone for the pitcher. The catcher's receiving hand or the glove position is the important point here. The glove should always *curl* toward the strike zone, not away. Remember, we are saying a *curl* or slight turn of the wrist toward the strike zone and not a quick pull or jerking motion. On high pitches, fingers curl down (Photo 3-4); on outside or inside pitches, the glove hand turns in (Photos 3-5 and 3-6) and on low pitches the hand and fingers curl up (Photo 3-7). The catcher works on this technique whenever he is receiving, whether in the bullpen or during batting practice. It is a technique that must become natural.

Photo 3-4

Photo 3-5

Photo 3-6

Photo 3-7

Giving Signs

There has to be a communication system between the catcher and the pitcher. This is done by giving signs. The first thing a catcher must be aware of is not letting any opponent steal his signs. He generally will have a different set of signs for each pitcher. One set of signs is when there are no runners on base, and the other is when there is a runner on second.

With no runners on base, the catcher can use a simple set of signs like holding out one finger for a fast ball, two fingers for a curve, and fluttering the fingers for a change of speed. If the catcher wants the pitch inside, he taps the inside thigh of the leg closest to the batter. If he wants the pitch outside, he taps the thigh of the outside leg. If the catcher wants the pitch up high, he can signal this by touching his chest protector after he has given his sign. If he wants the pitch low, he can touch his shin guard. With a runner on second, the catcher should use a different set of signs because the runner is looking right at him. He can flash three signs and use the second or third one for the actual sign. In doing this, it is a good idea to change the pattern after a few innings so the runners do not begin to figure out your system.

Tagging the Runner

There are two types of tags with which a catcher must be concerned. One is when a runner slides into home plate, and the other is when the runner tries to bowl him over, hoping to jar the ball loose. The important thing the catcher must do is to make sure he is facing the runner so he is protected by his equipment. When the catcher lines up the throw coming in, he plants his left foot on the front part of home plate. The catcher should show the runner the outside part of home plate so he will slide toward it. If the catcher shows the runner the outside part of home plate, he will slide rather than run into him. When he receives the ball, he holds it with two hands and tags the runner. If the runner tries to hit him, he holds the ball with two hands and tags him with a slight give as contact is made. Otherwise, if the catcher stands still and flat-footed, the runner will knock him over.

When tagging home on a force play, he catches the ball in front of him with his right foot on the plate so he can throw the ball quickly without taking an extra step. The main thing is to stretch out and reach the ball as quickly as he can.

Throws from the Outfield

Catching the ball is the important thing because the tag cannot be made without the ball. The catcher must do everything to get the ball for this purpose. We suggest that the catcher keep his mask on for all of the following because it offers him greater protection, not only against the runner, but against bad bounces. His vision should not be impaired in any way by the mask because he uses it to catch at all times. The catcher should position his feet in front of the plate facing the throw. When receiving a throw from left field, the catcher will show the runner the *outside part* of the plate, and quickly move his left foot to block that area of the plate after he catches the ball.

On throws from center, the catcher has his left foot placed midway in front of home plate, again showing the runner the outside part of the plate. The tagging and blocking are the same as from center field.

Throws from right field place the catcher closer to the right side of the plate, but you want him to again show the runner the outside part of the plate. Make sure your catcher is well aware of what he is showing the runner, so that he has only to be prepared to block that part of the plate. In all of these situations, you want your catcher to avoid having a collision; he must catch the ball and tag with the back portion of the glove with the ball securely in the bare hand. When there is contact, he should roll with it and try to regain his balance for further plays.

Catching the Pop-up

It takes a lot of hard practice to learn how to catch pop-ups. When the ball is popped up behind home plate, the spin of the ball will generally take it back toward the infield. The catcher should have his back toward the diamond so the ball will come toward him, rather than away from him. When the ball is popped up, the catcher takes his mask off and holds it in his hand until he locates the ball. When he sees it, he then throws his mask away, far enough that he doesn't step and trip over it. He should try and catch the ball with his glove up, just like an outfielder. If there is a pop-up in front of the plate, the catcher should listen for someone's call to take it. If an infielder can get it, let him take it.

Spin Over Right or Left Shoulder

On foul pop-ups, the catcher must turn in the direction that the ball has been hit. If the ball goes over his right shoulder, turn to the right; if the ball goes over his left shoulder, turn to the left. Drills with the coach hitting fungoes over the shoulder of the catcher and calling "left" or "right" would help the catcher get into a good habit. Follow up without calling left or right whenever the opportunity presents itself during batting practice; the catcher should incorporate the proper movements. Perfect practice makes perfect catchers!

Fielding Bunts (Photo 3-8)

In fielding bunts, the catcher must move out after the ball as quickly as possible. He should field all rolling bunts with two hands. He should place the glove out in front of the ball and scoop the ball into the glove with the throwing hand. He must make sure he has good control of the ball before he throws it, and never take his eyes off the ball until he is ready to throw it. If the catcher has time, he should throw the ball overhand; if he does not have time, he then has to throw it side arm like a quick-releasing infield throw.

Photo 3-8

THE PITCHER AND CATCHER—
AN ESSENTIAL RELATIONSHIP

The catcher must not overlook the psychological aspects of his position. He must always be aware of who is on the mound and what that pitcher is capable of doing on that particular day. The catcher must know what is usually the pitcher's best pitch. We use the word "usually" because we also realize that on a particular day the pitcher's best pitch may not be there, or the pitcher may not have it at the start of the game, or another pitch may be working better that day.

The relationship that develops between the catcher and his pitcher is one that is always being expanded. It starts in pre-season workouts, and continues whenever the pitcher is getting ready for a game (you want your starting catcher to get down to the bullpen and take the last five to eight minutes of the pitcher's warm-up). This gives the catcher the opportunity to see what is working well for the pitcher on that day. Strengths and weaknesses of the pitcher are handled by the catcher as he sees fit. Many times a smartly called game is only the result of experience, in which the catcher uses the pitcher's strengths to the maximum. Constant communication between catcher and pitcher keeps both on their toes and keeps results to their advantage.

The intelligent catcher will also use the pitcher's strengths where the umpire appreciates them the most. How often do you see catchers argue with umpires on certain pitches throughout the game? Instead, the intelligent catcher will tell his pitcher, "The umpire is calling them up here or down there for strikes; let's get the ball there." This is called "working the umpire's strike zone." Why fight with the umpire? Experience has taught the catcher that he is better off by joining him. He works with the umpire and doesn't say things that will cause him to become upset with the catcher and in turn, with the pitcher. An umpire is only human and the catcher must feel him out and work with him. This intelligent approach to the game will make the catcher a big asset to the pitcher and the team.

TIPS FOR THE CATCHER

1. Take charge; be the quarterback.
2. Check your fielders and see if they are in position.
3. Be sure to give the pitcher a good target.
4. On the intentional pass, keep one foot in the catcher's box until the pitcher releases the ball.
5. Learn your pitcher's most effective pitch.
6. Always be alert for any steal or hit-and-run situation.
7. Back up first base with the bases unoccupied on all batted balls that might result in overthrows.
8. Be sure to call "cut" if you want a ball cut off.
9. If a bunt is in order, call for high pitches.
10. Study the hitter's stance, and remember what he went after and where he hit the ball in previous appearances.
11. Make the signs simple and understandable.

SPOTTING HITTERS' WEAKNESSES

Young catchers should not concern themselves with trying to spot hitters' weaknesses until they have learned the proper mechanics of catching. As they are learning the tools of their trade, catchers should observe the batting mannerisms of all hitters. They will observe the stances that are used by different hitters and what these hitters can accomplish with the different pitches that they are thrown. In most situations a hitter's stance could reveal some flaw or overcompensation that he is making, and an experienced catcher will know when and where to take advantage of it.

The following are common reactions to the different stances that hitters could take:

- Keep the ball high and inside when a hitter crouches;
- Pitch the ball outside for the hitter who steps away from the plate;
- Keep the ball low for the upright or erect batter.

Pre-game batting practice will also allow the catcher to size up some of his opponents. Many times he can easily see the overstrider, the lunger, the hitcher, the foot-in-the-bucket, and the head-turner. The above faults and others may be handled in the following ways.

Fault	Pitch to Use
Stepping in bucket	Outside pitch
Hitching (hand)	Fast ball up
Lunging	Off speed, curve
Overstriding	High fast ball
	Keep ball inside
Dropping the rear shoulder	Inside pitches
Pulling the head	Breaking pitches
	Moving fast ball
Up in the box	Fast balls
Back in the box	Curves

The following checklist can be used as a quick check to make sure your catchers have covered the basics.

CHECKLIST FOR CATCHERS

Stance

_____ Has good signal position, which prevents offense from stealing signs, by keeping gloved hand over left knee, and signaling hand inside of right thigh.

_____ Receiving position is semi-erect to shift left or right and be ready to throw.

Receiving and Throwing

_____ Gets as close to the batter as possible when ready to receive the pitch.

_____ Knows proper method of catching pitch in the dirt.

_____ Has mastered the art of "framing," with the glove curling toward the strike zone rather than away.

Catching the Ball

_____ Use two hands whenever possible.

_____ Brings ball toward the middle of the body.

_____ Blocks bad pitches.

_____ Protects throwing hand.

_____ Shifts into throwing position.

Throwing

_____ Gets ball away quickly.

_____ Takes minimum number of steps.

_____ Throws overhand with quick, snappy release.

_____ Knows where and how to throw on a double steal.

Other

_____ Gives signals effectively.

_____ Knows proper way to tag runner.

_____ Catches foul and fly balls.

_____ Fields bunts.

_____ Hustles to back up first base whenever necessary.

_____ Returns ball to pitcher.

_____ Knows pitch-out procedure.

_____ Knows pickoff procedure.

_____ Studies the hitters.

_____ Sets up the hitters.

_____ Calls the play in a bunt situation.

DRILLS FOR CATCHERS

Stance Drill

Purpose: To acquaint the catcher with the proper stance and positions used during the game.

Description: The coaching staff will work with the catcher to acquaint him with the proper body positions: feet shoulder width apart, toes pointed straight ahead or slightly toed in, knees pointed straight ahead, and the backside low with the back leaning slightly forward (see Photo 3-2).

Remember, you, the coach, will acquaint the catcher with the proper arm and hand location, as well as the proper finger location.

Signal-Giving Drill

Purpose: To make sure the signs can be seen by the pitcher and not by the opposing team.

Description: Select members of the team in trying to pick off the catcher's signals; also, ask the pitcher if he knows what sign was given. The coach tells the catcher what signal to give to the pitcher; the pitcher tells the assistant coach what the signal was. Coaches make sure they are in agreement.

Throwing Drill

Purpose: To instruct the catcher in gripping the ball properly. Ball should be gripped across the seams at the widest part of the seams.

Description: Whenever the catcher is playing catch, he should quickly grip the ball across the seams. While catching, he can check his grip and try to increase the quickness that is required for a good release.

Backing Up Third

(Bunt Situation—Ball Bunted to Third Baseman)

Purpose: To show how it is the catcher's responsibility to move to third when there is a sacrifice bunt and the third baseman has fielded it.

Description: The catcher sees the third baseman fielding the bunt, and runs to cover third base. This will keep the runner at first base from advancing to third base.

Fielding Bunted Balls

Purpose: To instruct the catcher in the proper movements of fielding a bunted ball and to acquaint him with his responsibilities of taking charge.

Description:

1. The ball is rolled up the first or third base lines by the coach or the catcher. (The coach can be located behind the catcher so the catcher cannot anticipate the throw and must react.)
2. The catcher fields ball (properly) and throws to first base. (The coach corrects mechanics.)
3. When the second baseman, third baseman, and shortstop are added, the coach will roll or bunt ball. The catcher will direct players using verbal and pointing methods. (The coach will make corrections.)

Tagging Runners

Purpose: To instruct the catcher on how to show a part of the plate and how to block it when making a tag.

Description:

1. Position catcher for throws from the different outfield positions.
2. The catcher will show that part of the plate that *he wants*, then catch the ball and block the *plate*.
3. This is done with the coach showing the proper positioning of feet for throws from the outfield.
4. The coach can position himself approximately 90 feet away with fungo bat. He hits grounders to the catcher who is in full gear; the catcher must react, then catch the ball, and then block and tag an imaginary runner. The coach will fungo the ball from all different angles.

Movement on Ball in Dirt

(Directly in Front)

Purpose: To block the ball and to keep it in front and under control.

Description:

1. Catcher is in full gear.
2. Coach or another catcher or pitcher about 35 feet away.
3. Ball is thrown* in dirt in front of catcher.
4. Catcher drops to both knees (shin guards are now out of way).
5. Catcher places glove in middle and uses soft part of his body to keep the ball in front of him.
6. The catcher should try to keep his body square to the pitcher (shoulders and body).

Movement on Ball in Dirt

(Directly in Front, Runner or Runners on Base)

Purpose: To try to catch the ball cleanly.

Description:

1. Same as previous drill, except the catcher will try to catch the ball before it hits dirt. If he should miss, his body will still be in proper blocking position.
2. The second part of the drill is to have the catcher come up throwing on all fielded balls.
3. The coach makes corrections.

Blocking Balls in Dirt to Right or Left

Purpose: To instruct catcher in moving the leg on the side of the bad throw first.

Description:

1. Same as previous drill, except throws are to the right or the left.
2. The catcher moves the leg on the side of the bad throw first.
3. The movements of blocking and trying to catch the ball are used in this drill as well.
4. The coach will correct the glove position. (The back hand is used in this drill.)

---

*Fungo can also be used at slightly longer distances of up to 60 feet away.

Dropping Third Strike Drill

Purpose: To have the catcher and first baseman work together in having the ball thrown to first base with the least amount of obstruction. Catcher pretends or does drop pitched ball.

Description:

1. The first reaction is to pick up the ball and tag the batter, if possible.
2. Second reaction is to make the first baseman aware of where the catcher is throwing the ball—*inside* or *outside*. In most cases, this will result from where the ball might have rolled after the catcher dropped the third strike. (Again, it is important for the catcher and players to know when they are required to throw the batter out at first. Verbal communication is essential in this drill.)

Movement on Wide Pitches

Purpose: To demonstrate shifting on wide pitches.

Description:

1. Instruct in stepping with the outside foot, that is the foot on the side closest to where the ball is thrown.
2. Ball is thrown to right or left side of catcher by coach or other catcher.
3. The catcher steps to that side with the foot that is closest to the ball (lead foot).

Dropping the Third Strike

Purpose: To instruct in finding the dropped third strike and throwing properly to first base.

Description:

1. Coach throws the ball to the catcher.
2. Catcher catches the ball and looks to coach's hand as to where ball would be.
3. Catcher reacts by turning in direction of ball, fielding it, and throwing to first base. As he throws, he lets the first baseman know if the throw is to be inside or outside.
4. Coach instructs in proper fundamentals.

DRILLS ON DISCARDING MASK AND FIELDING GROUND BALLS

Force Play

Purpose: To learn proper footwork when catching a ball at the plate in a force-out situation.

Description:

1. Catcher and coach are about 25–30 feet apart.
2. Coach throws ball to plate.
3. Catcher receives ball with right foot on plate.
4. As the catcher receives the throw, he steps with his left foot and throws ball back to coach (first baseman).

Run Downs

Purpose: To instruct in running at a runner caught off base.

Description: See "Tagging the Runner" procedure.

Pop-ups

Purpose: To acquaint catcher with placing back to diamond on ball hit over his head.

Description:

1. Catchers should turn and locate the ball.
2. Discard the mask when ball is at its greatest height.
3. Catch ball with glove up in middle of forehead.
4. Coach should comment in terms of correct mechanics and reactions.

Gimmicks to hit pop-up:

1. Tennis racquet with rubber ball
2. Pitching machine

INFIELD PLAY:
Championship Techniques for Playing First, Second, Third, and Shortstop

To develop infield play, you must instruct your players in both mental and physical factors. Infielders need to know types of hitters, playing fields, and the basic situations. Let's familiarize ourselves and our players with such sound principles of the game.

WHAT INFIELDERS MUST KNOW

Knowledge of the Hitter

The infielder should know the type of hitter at the plate. Is he a pull hitter, opposite field hitter, spray hitter or a power hitter? As he gains experience, he should learn to judge a hitter's type from his stance at the plate, the way he holds the bat, and his practice swings. He should also know if the hitter is a fast, average, or slow runner.

Knowledge of Playing Conditions

The infielder should survey the ground conditions around his position before the game. He should know if the ground is hard, soft, fast, slow, wet or dry. Is it an "all skin" (no grass) infield? He should check the wind to see if it will have any effect on his position that day. Is the sun going to affect his position during any part of the ball game? All of these questions should be answered before the game begins, and as the game is played.

Anticipating the Play

During the game the infielder should know what pitch the pitcher is going to throw. He should also relay this information to his outfielders. The infielder should know the number of outs and especially be aware of game situations. He should be alert for possible hit-and-run situations, bunt or squeeze situations, or straight and delayed steal possibilities. The infielder must always be alert and should never be taken by surprise.

INFIELDER'S STANCE

The stance for the infielder should be comfortable. His feet should be approximately shoulder-width apart. The left foot should be slightly in front of the right foot. The weight should be evenly distributed on the balls of the feet. He should *not* be back on his heels. His body should be facing the hitter squarely. His hands should be resting on his knees, which are slightly bent, and he should be watching the pitcher.

As the pitcher is about to deliver the ball to the hitter, the infielder should remove his hands from his knees and take a short step with the left foot and then the right foot toward home plate (Photo 4-1). This is done in order to get his body in motion before the ball is hit. While he is taking the short step toward home plate he is following the flight of the ball from the pitcher's hand to home plate.

Photo 4-1

CATCHING, THROWING, AND FIELDING SKILLS

Catching a Thrown Ball

The fielder should always catch a thrown ball with two hands, and he should try to be directly in front of the ball when he catches it. The hands should be extended away from the body, with a slight bend at the elbows. Once the ball is in the glove, the hands should "give" (soft hands) and be brought into the body or into the throwing area.

Illustration 4-1

Illustration 4-2

To catch a ball above the waist, the palms should be turned away from the body and the hands placed in a position we call "thumb to thumb." (See Illustration 4-1.)

To catch a ball below the waist, the palms should be facing upward and the hands placed in a position we call "pinky to pinky." (See Illustration 4-2.)

Throwing the Ball

An infielder must be able to throw the ball from all positions (overhand, sidearm, and underhand). He must also learn to be fluid in his motion, not "herky-jerky."

After fielding the ball, the infielder should bring the ball to the center of his body (belt), remove the ball from the glove, and get the ball into throwing position. The front shoulder should be pointed directly at the player he is throwing to. Pointing the front toe, he should step with his stride leg directly at this same player. As the stride leg lands, the arm should start to come through and the upper part of the body should be square to the receiving player. We call this the "four corners." The top of both shoulders and the points of both hips are squarely facing the player to receive the ball. As the ball is released, the infielder should have a good follow-through. This will aid in getting velocity into the throw and, most importantly, it will aid his accuracy.

The infielder should grip the ball across the wide seams on the ball. The fingertips of the index and middle fingers should be touching the seam and the thumb should be beneath the ball and touching the seam also. As the ball is released, it will come off the index and middle fingers with backspin. We call this "four-seam rotation." The four-seam rotation will keep trajectory of the ball in a straight line, that is, the ball will not tail or slide to either side. This will make it easier for the player waiting to receive the ball to catch it.

Fielding a Ground Ball
Hit Directly at the Infielder

Once the ball is hit, the infielder should start to charge the ball and get his body under control in order to field the ball. The infielder should keep his body low, keep his eyes on the ball, and get his body directly in front of the ball. As he approaches the ball, he should have the left foot slightly in front of the right foot, hands away from the

Photo 4-2

body, and he should "look" the ball into the glove. The ball should be fielded in the center of the body, with the glove and throwing hand being together "pinky to pinky" and the arms, slightly bent, forming a "V" leading to the shoulders. The glove, arms, and shoulders should be considered a triangle in good fielding form (Photo 4-2).

As the infielder catches the ball, there should be a slight give of the hands (soft hands) and he should take the ball out of the glove with the throwing hand and get the ball into the throwing position as quickly as possible.

Photo 4-3

The infielder should take a "skip-step" or "crow-hop" to get himself into throwing position. He should step directly toward the receiving fielder and throw overhand whenever possible (Photo 4-3).

Fielding a Ground Ball
Hit to the Right

On a ball hit to the infielder's right, from the ready position, the infielder should use the crossover step. He should pivot on the right foot, cross over with the left foot, and slide his body in front of the ball. He should field the ball in the middle of his body and plant the right foot hard into the ground to stop his momentum (Photo 4-4). He should then take his skip step and throw. He can do this if he has the time. If there is a fast runner, then the infielder may have to plant the right foot and throw right from there.

If the infielder has to "back hand" the ball, he should try to plant the right foot and get rid of the ball as quickly as possible.

Photo 4-4

Fielding a Ball
Hit to the Left

The infielder should use the crossover step, pivot on the left foot, cross over with the right foot, and get the body directly in front of the ball and field the ball in the middle of the body. Now the infielder must get into position to throw.

In order to get into position to throw while going left, the infielder must use a "cross back-step." As the infielder fields the ball in the middle of his body, he should cross the right foot behind the left and plant it. This will stop his momentum and turn his body to where he is throwing. He should then step with the left foot directly to where he is throwing, open up the body to show the four corners, and follow through on the throw.

Fielding the Slow Hit Ball

The infielder should charge the ball and, as he approaches the ball, get his body under control. As he approaches the ball, his body should be approximately one step to the right of the ball. This will give him a better angle for throwing. He should field the ball with the glove as he comes across the ball. He should then step forward with the right foot and throw underhand off the right foot. The only time the ball should be fielded with the bare hand is when the ball is dead in the grass or almost completely stopped.

Fielding a Bobbled Ball

Once he has bobbled a ball, the infielder should not panic. He must remain calm, locate the ball, and get to it as quickly as possible. He should pick up the ball with his bare hand, because he will have more control with the bare hand than he will with the glove. Once he picks up the ball, he should not put it back into the glove, as this wastes time. He should bring the ball immediately to the throwing position.

In order to pick up the ball with his bare hand, the infielder should use his hand as a "three-pronged tool." The prongs are the index, middle, and ring fingers, while the thumb and pinky go to the other side of the ball. The infielder should try to push the ball into the ground. He should not try to get the fingers under the ball. Actually, what the infielder is doing is going after the ball with the three fingers and he comes up throwing with two fingers.

GENERAL INFIELD POSITIONING

Normal Depth

This is where the infielder will play most hitters. He will change this position according to the game situation or the hitter.

Infield In

This position is usually at the edge of the infield grass. The infielder should be ready to make the out at home plate. This is the most precarious position for the infielder because it limits his range, and balls that are hit hard, not directly at the infielder, usually get through.

Infield Halfway

This is your usual double-play positioning. The shortstop and second baseman move approximately eight to ten feet in from their normal position and eight to ten feet closer to second base. The first and third basemen are approximately five to eight feet behind the base. Also from this position, on a hard-hit ball directly at an infielder, it is possible to make a play on a runner at home plate.

Infield Deep

All infielders play as deep as possible. The shortstop and second baseman play on the edge of the outfield grass, or deeper if the speed of the runner allows. The first and third basemen should be fifteen to twenty feet behind the base. The infielders are trying to get more range and keep the ball in the infield.

Split Infield

The shortstop and second baseman play in double-play depth and the third and first basemen play even with the bases. From this positioning the shortstop and second baseman can make a play at home plate or turn the double play. The third and first basemen can also make a play at home plate or go for the double play.

INDOOR INFIELD DRILLS

Improving Proper Footwork
in Fielding a Ground Ball

An infielder stands on a line and gets into his proper stance for fielding a ground ball. A coach stands in the middle of the floor with a bag of balls next to him. The coach rolls a ball five to ten feet to the left of the infielder. The infielder must use a crossover step and get in front of the ball and allow it to go through his legs. A glove is not used for this drill. The object of the drill is to get the infielder in front of the ball in good fielding position with the proper leg work. If the ball goes directly through his legs, it shows he has gotten in front of the ball. The coach keeps rolling balls to the infielder's left until he comes to the end of the line. The drill is now repeated to the right side of the infielder.

Quick Hands

Two infielders rest on their knees facing one another about fifteen to twenty feet away. Each infielder throws different types of bounces to the other in order to quicken the hands in catching the ball. This drill enables the infielders to react to the different types of hops from which the ball can be caught.

Opening Up to Throwing Side on a Relay Throw

Three infielders spread out the length of the gym. One infielder throws the ball to the man in the middle. When the middle man receives the throw he gets into the proper body position by opening himself to his throwing side to relay the throw to the next man. The infielder receiving the next throw practices his tag.

The drill starts over with the player who received the last throw. After about four or five relay throws the infielders switch positions.

THE FIRST BASEMAN

Qualifications

The first baseman should be tall and agile. He should have quick hands and feet and should be able to field ground balls and take throws. It is preferable if the first baseman is left-handed. Being left-handed makes it easier for him to field bunts and throw to third base. It is also much easier to throw to second base on the 3-6-3 double play. Ideally, a first baseman should also hit with some power.

Positioning

Deep. The first baseman should normally play at the edge of the outfield grass and wide of the base. This will enable him to cover the most ground.

Halfway. The first baseman should move halfway between the outfield grass and first base. This position should be used when there is a slight possibility of a bunt or a hitter at home plate with better than average speed.

Holding the runner on. The first baseman should take a position to hold the runner on any time second base is unoccupied, unless the game situation dictates otherwise.

Bunt situation—play on grass. The first baseman should play on the infield grass in a bunt situation with runners on first and second base. He is responsible for fielding any ball bunted behind the pitcher, who is breaking toward the third-base foul line in order to be in a position to field a bunt and throw to third base.

Awaiting the throw. When a ball is hit to another infielder, the first baseman must get to first base as quickly as possible. He should face the infielder who is making the throw. His hands should be held chest high. This is the target for the infielder. The first baseman should have his feet spread approximately shoulder-width apart and his heels two to three inches away from the base. The first baseman will then shift his feet to catch the ball after the infielder releases the ball.

Catching

The first baseman should catch the ball *with two hands* whenever possible.

Catching balls thrown to the infield side of first base

A right-handed first baseman should shift his feet to the inside of first base and touch the base with the right foot on a ball that is thrown to the infield side of the base.

A left-handed first baseman should touch first base with the left foot, cross over with the right foot and reaches for the ball with the glove hand.

Catching balls thrown to the outfield side of first base

A right-handed first baseman, on a throw to the outfield side of first base, touches first base with the right foot, crosses over with the left and reaches for the ball with the glove hand.

A left-handed first baseman shifts his feet, touches the base with his left foot and reaches for the ball with the glove hand.

Catching balls thrown in the dirt

The general rule for balls in the dirt is to make sure that the first baseman blocks the ball. Do not let the ball get by and let the runner advance another base.

Scoop (short hop). The first baseman should stretch to reach the ball. A right-handed first baseman keeps the right foot in contact with the base. A left-handed first baseman keeps the left foot in contact with the base. The first baseman should try to catch the ball at the closest point of contact with the ground.

Remember, do not stretch until the ball is released by the other infielder. By stretching too soon, the first baseman cuts down on his ability to move or shift with the throw.

Long hop. The first baseman should keep his body erect and let the ball come to him on the big hop. Do not stretch for the ball.

In-between hop. The first baseman should back up slightly (shoulders hunched over and weight slightly forward). He should stay on the infield side of the base and make sure he blocks the ball with his body.

Catching the high throw. The first baseman should step on top of the base to get added height in receiving the throw. The right-handed first baseman steps on the base with the right foot and the left-handed first baseman steps on the base with the left foot. After receiving the throw, the first baseman should step into foul territory to avoid a collision with the runner.

Leaving first base to catch the ball. If the first baseman cannot keep his foot on the base and reach the ball, then he must get off the base in order that the ball does not get past him. If the throw is to the inside of the diamond (up the first base foul line), the first baseman should come off the base and try to make a sweeping tag on the runner as he goes by.

Fielding

Throwing to second base

During infield practice, the first baseman should always make the play as he would during a game. A left-handed first baseman should throw from where he fields the ball. A right-handed first baseman should always turn inside toward second base, straighten up and throw. The first baseman should never turn his back to the infield. All throws to second base should be made quickly. It is not how hard the ball is thrown, but the quickness and accuracy that counts. The lead runner must be retired to assure the double play. The first baseman should always throw at the shortstop's face.

If the first baseman is playing deep behind first base, then his throw should be to the outside (outfield) side of second base. If the first baseman is playing in or holding a runner on, he should throw to the inside (infield) side of second base.

Feeding the ball to the pitcher covering first base

On a ground ball to first base which is fielded by the first baseman, he should make the play unassisted whenever possible. Only when he cannot beat the runner to first base should he make the play to the pitcher covering. The throw to the pitcher should be a soft, underhand, stiff-wristed toss about chest high. The ball should be fielded, and the first baseman should be moving toward first base. He should take the ball out of the glove and toss it to the pitcher before he reaches first base. If the pitcher receives the ball before he reaches first base, then the only thing he has to be concerned with is touching the base. If he receives the ball at the same time he reaches first base, then he must be concerned with catching the ball, touching first base and avoiding the oncoming runner.

Positioning with runners on base

Runner on first base only. The first baseman should hold the runner on in this case. His right foot should be placed on the inside corner of first base. He should have his body angled so as to be in position to take a pickoff throw from the pitcher (Photo 4-5). As the pitcher delivers the ball to home plate, the first baseman should step into the diamond with the left foot, and cross over with the right foot. This will put the first baseman in a position squarely facing home plate. He is now in position to react to any ball hit in his direction.

Runners on first and second base (bunt situation). The first baseman should play on the infield grass (not holding the runner on). He should charge toward home plate with the pitch and look to make the play at third base.

Runners on first and second base (no bunt situation). The first baseman should play behind the runner and be ready to make a double play (3-6-3 or 3-6-1).

Photo 4-5

Tagging. Tagging is much easier for a left-handed first baseman because his glove hand is closer to first base. The right-handed first baseman must reach across his body to make a tag. The tag should be quick and sweeping. The glove should be swept across the inside portion of first base.

Popflies. The first baseman should use his voice to call for the ball. He should take charge on any balls hit between the catcher and the first baseman and also between the pitcher and first baseman. On foul fly balls near the stands or fence, the first baseman should get to the fence first and then can drift back toward the infield. If he drifts to the fence, he will be looking for the fence and can lose sight of the ball.

Topped balls. On all topped balls in fair territory in front of home plate, the first baseman should give his target in fair territory. He should place his left foot on first base and stretch into the diamond. On a passed ball in foul territory (first-base line), he should give his target in foul territory. He should place his right foot on the base and stretch into foul territory.

Cutoffs. The first baseman is the cutoff man on all balls hit to center field and right field. On all balls hit that are sure doubles or possible triples, the first baseman steps inside the diamond to make sure the batter–runner touches first base. He then follows the runner to second base in case the runner rounds second base.

If the ball is cut off and thrown behind the runner at second base, it is the first baseman who will make the play.

Fielding bunts. With a runner on first base the first baseman must hold the runner on. When the pitcher delivers the ball to home plate, he charges and has the responsibility of fielding any bunt along the first-base line. He should listen to the catcher, who will determine where the throw will be made. Remember, you must get an out in this situation.

With runners on first and second base, the first baseman positions himself 10 to 15 feet in front of first base on the infield grass. He should charge as the pitcher delivers the ball to home plate and he has the responsibility of fielding any ball bunted along the first-base line or behind the pitcher. He listens for the catcher to tell him where to throw. *Remember*, you must get an out in this situation.

Tips for the First Baseman

1. Be quick with the first three or four steps. Ninety percent of the balls fielded by him will be within the three or four step range.
2. Take the play unassisted whenever possible.
3. Always protect the line in the late innings. Any ball hit between the line and the first baseman is usually good for extra bases.
4. Get off the base to block errant throws. Don't let the ball get by.
5. Two good rules to follow on balls hit to the right of first base:

   "If it's hot, take a shot."

   "If it's slow, let it go."
6. Watch the hitter while the ball is being pitched. The first baseman will get a better jump on the ball and pick up the batter attempting to bunt the ball much quicker.

THE THIRD BASEMAN

Qualifications

The third baseman must have quick reactions and a good pair of hands. He must have a strong arm. He must also have a strong chest, since he has to block everything. Even if he can't make the catch, if he can knock the ball down, he has the chance to throw out the runner.

Positions

Deep. The third baseman should play seven or eight steps behind third base and four to five steps off the foul line. This position will give him the greatest range.

Normal. The third baseman should play approximately three or four steps away from third base and one or two steps behind third base.

In (bunt situation). The third baseman should play two or three steps in front of third base on the infield grass. The third baseman should play close to the foul line in the late innings of a close ball game.

Fielding

Fielding a ground ball. The third baseman must be quick in his first three or four steps. Ninety percent of the ground balls fielded by him will be in the range of three or four steps. He should use the crossover step on ground balls hit to the left or right of him. He should try to get his body in front of every ground ball. If he knocks the ball down, he still has the opportunity to throw out the runner.

Throwing. The third baseman should throw overhand whenever possible, although he must be able to throw from all positions (sidearm, underhand, etc.).

Tagging. The third baseman should straddle third base and make a sweep tag with the back of the glove. He should practice making a tag on all throws during infield and outfield practice to gain quickness.

Popflies. The third baseman should take all popflies between the catcher and third base and anything hit toward the third-base side of the pitcher's mound.

On foul popflies near the fence or stands, he should get to the fence as quickly as possible and then drift back into the infield to catch the ball.

Bunt situations. With a runner on first base, the third baseman positions himself about two or three steps on the infield grass. As the pitcher releases the ball toward home plate, the third baseman charges. He should circle into the ball, field the ball with two hands, and listen for the catcher to tell him where to throw. *Remember*; you must get an out in this situation.

With runners on first and second base, the third baseman positions himself two or three steps on the infield grass. In this situation, the third baseman must know the fielding capabilities of the pitcher. If the pitcher, who is charging the third-base foul line, can handle the bunt, then the third baseman retreats to third base and acts as a first baseman. If the bunt is hard and cannot be handled by the pitcher, then the third baseman must charge the bunt and make the play. If the bunt is very hard, the third baseman may have the option of going for the double play. The shortstop would be covering second base in this situation. *Remember*; you must get an out in this situation.

With a runner on second base only, everything is the same as with runners on first and second base. The only difference is that the play at third base is now a tag play, not a force out.

On a squeeze play, as the runner breaks from third base, the third baseman should yell "squeeze" and charge as hard as he can toward home plate.

Photo 4-6

Fielding topped balls and bunts. The third baseman should field all balls with the glove whenever possible. *Key:* If the ball is moving, field it with the glove. If the ball is stopped, field it barehanded.

In fielding the ball with the bare hand, the third baseman should charge the ball by rounding into it. He should keep his head down and his body low. He should cup his hand in order to get his fingers under the ball. He should field the ball with his left foot forward, take one step with the right foot and throw off the right foot to first base (Photo 4-6). The throw will be underhand and across his body. The throw should be aimed to the inside of the diamond as an underhand throw has a tendency to dip and tail into the baseline.

Cutoffs. The third baseman is the cutoff man on all throws to home plate from left field. If he is going to let the ball go through to the catcher at home plate, he should always fake the cutoff in order to freeze any other runners on base.

Tips for the Third Baseman

1. Always watch the hitter, especially his hands, in order to see bat angle and attempted bunts.
2. On balls hit directly back to the pitcher, always break toward the middle of the infield in order to be in position to field deflected balls.
3. Always pick up a bobbled ball with your bare hand.

THE SHORTSTOP

Qualifications

This is the toughest infield position to play, therefore, the shortstop should be your best infielder. He should be agile, have quick reflexes, and quick hands and feet. The shortstop must have a strong arm in order to make the play deep in the hole. If he does not have a strong arm, he must have the ability to get rid of the ball quickly.

Positioning

Deep. The shortstop should play as deep as possible to give himself the best possible chance to reach any ball hit in his direction. He may be able to take a step or two back on the outfield grass if there is a slow runner, or he may have to take a step or two closer to home plate if there is a fast runner at home plate.

Halfway (double-play position). The shortstop must cheat in toward home plate and closer to second base. A good rule of thumb to use in determining the cheating position is to move three steps toward home plate and three steps closer to second base. The most important factor involved in the cheating position is that the shortstop must be able to reach the base, set himself, and await the throw. He should not have to receive the throw while running at full speed.

In. The shortstop should play on the edge of the infield grass. He should be ready to make the play to home plate.

Fielding

Ground ball hit to the left. The shortstop, reacting from his ready position, should use the crossover step to get him into a position where he can field the ball directly in front of his body. After he has fielded the ground ball he takes a crossback step to turn his body so he is facing the first baseman as he makes his throw.

Ground ball hit to the right. The shortstop, reacting from his ready position, should use the crossover step, move toward the ball and slide the body in front of the ball and plant on the right foot. By planting on the right foot, he is stopping his momentum from going away from where he wants to throw. After planting the right foot, he should push off, take a skip step, and throw to first base.

Slow hit ball. The shortstop should charge the ball and get his body under control as he approaches the ball. He should circle into the ball if possible. Circling into the ball means that as he approaches the ball he should be one step to the right of the ball. By doing this, he gains a better angle in which to throw to first base. He should field the ball with the left foot forward, take a step with the right foot and throw underhand (across his body) to first base.

Popflies. The shortstop should take all popflies in the infield that he can reach. The shortstop has priority over the third baseman on any popfly that the third baseman has to back up to catch. He should attempt to catch any popfly in short left field or centerfield until called off by one of the outfielders.

THE SECOND BASEMAN

Qualifications

A second baseman must have quick hands and feet. He should be adept at fielding all types of ground balls and have the ability to get rid of the ball quickly and from any angle. He must have the ability to make the pivot on the double play. A strong arm is not a prime consideration in choosing a second baseman, because most of his throws will be short.

Positioning

Deep. The second baseman should play to give himself the best possible chance to reach any ball hit in the direction of second base. He may be able to take a step or two back on the outfield grass if there is a slow runner, or he may have to take a step or two closer to home plate if there is a fast runner at home plate.

Halfway (double-play position). The second baseman must cheat in toward home plate and closer to second base. A good rule of thumb to use in determining the cheating position is to move three steps toward home plate and three steps closer to second base. The most important factor involved in the cheating position is that the second baseman must be able to reach the base, set himself, and await the throw. He should not have to receive the throw while running at full speed.

In. The second baseman should play on the edge of the infield grass. He is looking to make the play to home plate.

Fielding

Ground ball hit to the left. The second baseman, reacting from his ready position, should use the crossover step to get him into a position where he can field the ball directly in front of his body. After he has fielded the ground ball he takes a crossback step to turn his body so he is facing the first baseman as he makes his throw.

The crossover step. From the ready position (Photo 4-7), the fielder pivots on the left foot (Photo 4-8) (without lifting the foot), and crosses over with the right foot (Photo 4-9). To go to the right, he pivots on the right foot and crosses over with the left.

Photo 4-7

Photo 4-8

Photo 4-9

Back-cross step. This step is used to help the infielder get his body under control and into throwing position after fielding the ball. The infielder should field the ball in the center of his body, and then drop the right foot behind the left with the weight transferring onto the right leg. The infielder uses the right foot to push off and steps with the left foot toward first base to make his throw. By using the back-cross step, the infielder cuts down on the number of steps he has to take in order to throw the ball.

Ground ball hit to the right. The second baseman, reacting from his ready position, should use the crossover step, move toward the ball, and slide the body in front of the ball and plant on the right foot. By planting on the right foot, he is stopping his momentum from going away from where he wants to throw. After planting the right foot, he should push off, take a skip step, and throw to first base.

Fielding a slow hit ball. The second baseman should charge the ball and get his body under control as he approaches the ball. He should circle into the ball if possible. Circling into the ball means that as he approaches the ball he should be one step to the right of the ball. By doing this, he gains a better angle in which to throw to first base. He should field the ball with the left foot forward, take a step with the right foot, and throw underhand (across his body) to first base.

Tagging. If time permits, the second baseman should try to straddle second base and receive the throw at a point directly above the base. He should wait for the ball to arrive. *Note:* The ball can travel faster to that point than the fielder reaching for it and bringing it back for the tag.

Popflies. The second baseman should attempt to catch all popflies around the second base area and behind first base when the first baseman must back up to catch the ball. He should also attempt to catch all popflies in short centerfield and right field until he is called off by either the shortstop or one of the outfielders.

Tips for Taggers

1. Make all tags with back of glove hand.
2. Keep hands relaxed.
3. Get in the habit of being an aggressive and quick tagger.

4. Make quick, sweeping tags.

5. Never leave the glove hand down in front of the base.

6. Let the runner come to the base. Don't reach out to make the tag. If you reach out, a good slider may evade the tag.

7. Never retag. If the tag is missed, the runner may still be called out.

8. Be alert for the runner oversliding the base.

9. Make sure the umpire has called the play before tossing the ball to a fellow player.

10. After making a tag, be ready to throw to another base for a continuing play.

TIPS FOR INFIELDERS

1. Think ahead.

2. Look for the ball to be hit to you on every play.

3. Have a comfortable stance, be well-balanced, and face the hitter squarely.

4. Use the cross-over step on balls hit to the right or left.

5. Have your body under control as you approach the ball.

6. Always get at least one out on a ground ball.

7. Know your pop-up priorities.

8. Don't make unnecessary throws.

9. Hustle after a bobbled ball and pick it up bare-handed.

10. Give the outfielder a target with the glove when acting as a relay man.

THE DOUBLE PLAY:
The Pitcher's Best Friend

5

The execution of the double play is the most important play in baseball. If you do not have a good double-play combination, you will not win many close games.

The shortstop and second baseman must be a team within a team. They should be the best of friends. They should almost be inseparable. They must know each other's thoughts, reactions, abilities, and shortcomings. In all practices, the shortstop and second baseman should play catch together, play pepper together, and, on road trips, they should even room together.

BASIC PRINCIPLES

In order to make the double play, there are a few basic principles that must be followed. First, you cannot make the double play unless the infielders "cheat" or "shade the bag." This means that both the shortstop and second baseman must give up ground and move closer to second base and also move closer to the hitter. A good rule of thumb is to move three steps closer to second base and three steps toward the hitter. Our feeling is that you must make the double play on the ball hit toward the middle. The ball hit in the hole, most of the time, will result only in the force at second base.

Second, the player who is on the pivot end of the double play must get to the base as quickly as possible. He must approach the base with both hands held chest high, giving his partner a target, and he must have his body under control. In this way, if the throw is bad, he can adjust and make sure of the first out. *Remember;* you can't make a double play if you don't get the lead man.

PIVOTS BY THE SHORTSTOP

The shortstop has three basic pivots that he can use. The first is the one most widely taught. The shortstop will round into the base with

Photo 5-1

Photo 5-2

Photo 5-3

Photo 5-4

his hands held high to give a target to the fielder who is making the initial throw. (See Photo 5-1.) He should have his body under control as he approaches the base. He should place his right foot (Photo 5-2) just behind the corner of the base and drag the foot across the base (Photo 5-3) with his momentum taking him toward first base (Photo 5-4).

Photo 5-5

Photo 5-6

Photo 5-7

The second pivot should be used when taking a throw from the first baseman, who is holding the runner on or who fields a ball on the infield grass. The shortstop should round into the base and get his body under control with hands held high, but this time he should position himself on the third base side of second base (Photo 5-5). When the throw is made, he should place his left foot (Photo 5-6) on the inside portion of the base and step into the infield to complete the throw to first base (Photo 5-7).

The third pivot is for the shortstop, who fields the ball close enough to second base so he can take the play himself. As the shortstop fields the ball, usually within *two* or *three* steps from second base (Photo 5-8), he should have some verbal communication with the second baseman. The shortstop can say, "I've got it," or the second baseman can say, "Take it yourself." The shortstop then continues to the base (Photo 5-9). As he sets up to throw, he places his left foot on the back of the base (Photo 5-10) and throws to first base. He uses the base as protection between himself and the runner (Photo 5-11).

Photo 5-8

Photo 5-9

Photo 5-10

Photo 5-11

PIVOTS BY THE SECOND BASEMAN

The pivot from the second base side is a little more difficult because the second baseman has his back to the runner and cannot see him. Many double plays are not completed because the second baseman hears footsteps, so to speak. The second baseman must possess some degree of courage to take the throw and make his throw to first base without being concerned about being taken out of the play by a sliding baserunner. For this reason, we try to teach a variety of pivots to the second baseman so that no matter where the feed is, he will have some means of avoiding the incoming runner.

The first pivot we teach is the one we feel is the easiest for the second baseman to learn and it also takes him away from the path of the runner. The second baseman's approach to the base is the same as that of the shortstop. He must round into the base (Photo 5-12), hands held high as a target for the player making the feed, and keep his body under control as he reaches the base.

As the throw is made, the second baseman should be one step behind the base. The second baseman should place his right foot to the left field side behind the base (Photo 5-13) and the left foot should cross over the base. As the second baseman catches the ball he should drag the right foot across the back corner of the base (Photo 5-14), take

Photo 5-12

Photo 5-13

Photo 5-14

a skip step, and throw to first base. By taking the skip step, the second baseman will get himself into the diamond and out of the way of the incoming runner.

On the next pivot, the second baseman places the left foot on top of the base (Photo 5-15). He catches the ball and comes across the base, lands on his right foot (Photo 5-16), and throws to first base (Photo 5-17).

Photo 5-15

Photo 5-16

Photo 5-17

On the next pivot, the second baseman places the left foot on the base, (Photo 5-18) receives the ball and pushes back off the base (Photo 5-19). He lands on the right foot and throws to first base.

The next pivot is the straddle. To use this a second baseman must have a strong arm. The second baseman gets to the base as

Photo 5-18   Photo 5-19

quickly as possible and straddles the bag (Photo 5-20). As he receives the throw (Photo 5-21) he touches the front of the base with the left toe and throws to first base (Photo 5-22). After making this pivot, the second baseman must remember not to be a spectator, but to get out of the way of the incoming runner.

Photo 5-20

Photo 5-21   Photo 5-22

The last pivot is used on a hard hit ball where there is no chance of the base runner taking out the second baseman. The second baseman gets to the base as quickly as possible and plants the right foot on the inside portion of the base (Photo 5-23). The second baseman then receives the ball, pushes off on the right foot, and throws to first base (Photo 5-24).

The double play must be worked on constantly until the execution becomes almost automatic. The only way to perfect it is with continuous practice.

Photo 5-23   Photo 5-24

FEEDS FROM THE SHORTSTOP
ON THE DOUBLE PLAY

Underhand Toss

The underhand toss should be used when the shortstop fields the ball close to second base. The ground ball should be fielded while moving toward second base with the left foot forward. As the ball is fielded and taken out of the glove, the shortstop pivots on the left foot and steps toward second base with the right foot. The toss is made while the shortstop is stepping toward second base with the right foot. The ball should be taken out of the glove in order to give the second baseman a good view of where the ball is coming from.

The toss should be made from just off the right hip (Photo 5-25). The toss should be stiff-wristed and underhand. Do not let the arm follow through any higher than the shoulder (Photo 5-26). The throw should have no arch to it and should be aimed directly at the second baseman's chest. After tossing the ball, the shortstop should continue his motion toward second base. *Remember*, the shortstop must take the ball out of the glove to give the second baseman a clear view of the ball.

Photo 5-25

Photo 5-26

Backhand Toss

The backhand toss is used when the ball is fielded far to the left and behind second base (Photo 5-27). This is also a stiff-wristed, forearm toss (Photo 5-28). The toss should be made while the weight is on the left foot (Photo 5-29). The toss should be aimed at the third base side of second base, which will allow the second baseman to complete his pivot.

Photo 5-27

Photo 5-28

Photo 5-29

Sidearm Toss (open up)

This toss is used on any ball that the shortstop can charge and get his body completely in front of (Photo 5-30). The ball should be fielded with the right foot slightly in front of the left foot. This allows the left hip to open up and the throw be made easily. If the ball is fielded with the left foot forward, then the left hip would be locked and the shortstop would have to throw across his body. As the shortstop makes the throw to second base, his weight is on the right foot and he pivots on the balls of his feet (Photo 5-31). The ball should be thrown from where it is fielded. The shortstop should not straighten up.

Photo 5-30

Photo 5-31

Sidearm Toss (Slide in the Plant)

Photo 5-32

Photo 5-33

This toss is used on any ball hit to the shortstop's right where he can get in front of the ball, but cannot charge it (Photo 5-32). The shortstop should get his body in front of the ball and slide on the right foot and plant it hard into the ground. As he plants the right foot (puts all the weight on the right foot), he opens the front hip and throws right from where he fields the ball to the second baseman. (See Photo 5-33.) *Remember:*

1. Open up the left hip to help in making the throw.
2. Do not hide the ball in the glove when throwing to second base.
3. Stay low and do not straighten up.

Backhand Play

After fielding the ball in the backhand position (Photo 5-34), the shortstop should take one more step with the right foot. He then should plant on the right foot (Photo 5-35), open the left hip, and throw to second base. He should make sure of an accurate throw to second base because he probably will only get one out on this play.

Photo 5-34

Photo 5-35

FEEDS FROM THE SECOND BASEMAN ON THE DOUBLE PLAY

Underhand Toss

The underhand toss is used on balls hit to the second baseman's right and close to the base. As the second baseman fields the ball in the center of his body, he pivots on the right foot and steps toward the base with the left foot. The ball should be taken out of the glove and fed to the shortstop with a stiff-wristed, underhand toss (Photo 5-36). Do not let the arm follow through any higher than the shoulder. The

Photo 5-36

throw should not have any arc to it and should be aimed directly at the shortstop's chest. The second baseman should continue his motion toward second base after releasing the ball. *Remember*, take the ball out of the glove in order to give the shortstop a good look at the ball.

Backhand Flip

This can be used instead of the underhand toss. It should be used only on a ball hit to the second baseman's right and one that he can get his body completely in front of. The toss should be no further than 20 feet

Photo 5-37

from second base. This is also a stiff-wristed forearm flip. The ball should be taken out of the glove and fed to the shortstop with the elbow and hand parallel with the ground. The palm of the hand is facing the shortstop (Photo 5-37). The ball should be pushed in a backhand manner toward the shortstop's chest. The ball should have very little or no spin at all and there should be no arc to the ball. It should be tossed on a line. After tossing the ball, the second baseman should continue his motion toward second base to complete the follow-through. This continuation of his motion will aid in the accuracy of the throw.

Jump Turn

This should be used when the second baseman is too far from second base to use the underhand toss or backhand flip. The ball should be fielded directly in front of the body with both hands. As the ball is caught, the second baseman should turn his entire body toward second base by means of a jump. As he jumps, he plants on the right foot and throws to second base. The second baseman should not straighten up to throw. The throw is the same as throwing a dart (right from the shoulder). See Photo 5-38.

Photo 5-38

Pivot in Tracks

This throw can be used in place of the jump turn. This throw can be used at a distance of 20 to 25 feet from second base. If thrown any further, the jump turn should be used in order to get more velocity on the throw. To get into position to make this type of throw, the second baseman should field the ground ball directly in front of him with the left foot slightly ahead of the right. As he catches the ball, he should pivot on the balls of the feet (turn his toes directly toward second base) and pivot at the hips so that the upper part of his body (chest) is facing second base squarely. See Photo 5-39.

He can go to his left knee when making a dart-type throw (right from the shoulder). This turn and throw will eventually be much quicker than the jump turn, but it takes more practice.

Photo 5-39

BALLS HIT TO THE EXTREME LEFT OF THE SECOND BASEMAN

This play is the only time a player should turn his back on the target to which he is throwing. As the second baseman fields the ball with his glove hand outstretched and his momentum going away from second base (Photo 5-40), he should take one more step with the right foot, which will turn his back to the infield. He should plant on the right foot and throw overhand to second base (Photo 5-41). The throw should be aimed chest high to the shortstop, who is positioned to the outfield side of second base. All of these feeds should be used during the course of a practice session so the shortstop and second baseman get used to working with each other.

Photo 5-40

Photo 5-41

TEACHING DOUBLE-PLAY SKILLS WITH THE PADDLE DRILL

An excellent way to teach all players, especially beginning players, to catch with two hands is to use a wooden paddle (Photo 5-42) with a glove stapled or tacked to one side (Photo 5-43). Have two players play catch, with one or both wearing paddles, at a distance of up to 20 to 25 feet. The paddle forces the player to catch with two hands, and to use a slight "give" in his hands when receiving the ball. This slight give of the hands is known as "soft hands."

We often use the glove-paddle when the shortstop and second baseman practice the double play. By using the glove-paddle to receive the feed at second base, the shortstop or the second baseman is forced to catch the ball with two hands (Photo 5-44), use "soft hands" and catch the ball in the center of his body.

Photo 5-42

Photo 5-43

Photo 5-44

OUTFIELD PLAY:
Hitting Versus Fielding Skills

6

"Speed in center, power hitting in left, strong arm in right." Is this all you want in your outfield? How often have you heard this approach or, better still, how often have you used this approach in getting individuals into the outfield line-up? Let's not argue for or against this approach, but let's look at all the fielding qualifications and skills necessary to play the outfield properly.

Every individual who steps on the outfield grass should be drilled in the skills essential for good performance. You can only teach and coach the skills; some individuals will possess more skills and ability to react than others. You can only use the appropriate drills to help develop the necessary skills.

QUALIFICATIONS:
THE BASIC FOUR

Let's look at our list of qualifications, often referred to as the basic four:

1. *Concentration.* The ability to focus on the pitcher and the batter is an ideal starting point for outfielders. The key to good outfield play is the ability to react, and good reaction time is a direct result of total concentration. We have all seen a game where the attention of one of the outfielders has wandered. He has not been tested throughout the contest and suddenly he is called upon to make a defensive play; he reacts with a late jump, the ball gets by him, and perhaps the game is over, too. As coaches, it is your responsibility to prepare the outfielders to be ready every moment, and it begins with the development of concentration.

2. *Speed.* The ability to get to the ball quickly is an asset. You want the outfielders to cover their territory, especially if the field is not fenced in. Center is usually the place for the quickest outfielder; he is responsible for cutting off the shots into the gaps.

3. *Strong throwing arm.* The ability to throw long and accurately is another important qualification for any outfielder. Getting the ball back to the infield quickly and accurately will keep many a runner from advancing.

4. *Knowledge of the situation.* Throwing to the wrong base or trying a "shoe-top" catch at the wrong time has cost us all a game or two. Outfielders must be constantly aware of the following: what? where? when? how? This simply means: *What* is the score? *Where* are the runners? He must know *when* and *how* to charge the ball, and *where* he should be to be prepared to make the primary and secondary throws.

Outfielder's Stance

The basic stance of the outfielder should be facing home plate squarely, with his feet comfortably apart at shoulder width, and his weight evenly distributed. His eyes should be focused on the pitcher and he should zero in on the batter as the delivery is made to the plate. As the pitcher delivers the ball, the outfielder's weight should come forward slightly and his arms should be in front of his body.

We emphasize this basic parallel stance because we believe it is easier to adjust from this foot position to others that might be better suited for each individual outfielder. The drop-step is taught as an essential skill for good movement by an outfielder.

Positioning

Let's look at some of the basic reactions and moves of the feet when a ball is hit:

Directly in front and on a short drive. The outfielder's initial *charge step* forward can be with either foot.

Short drive to right or directly to the right. The outfielder should take a *crossover step* with the left foot as his first reaction (Photo 6-1). The movement gives him the luxury of saving distance and time in getting to the ball.

Photo 6-1   Photo 6-2

Short drive to left or directly to the left. The outfielder makes his first movement the *crossover* with the right foot.

Balls hit deep to the right, left or directly overhead. The initial step (Photo 6-2) is a drop step back to the side to which the ball is hit. When the ball is hit directly at the outfielder, the drop step is usually with the foot on the glove side. Drills are essential in helping your players master these movements; they should emphasize quickness and getting to the ball.

Fly balls. In catching fly balls, your players should always try to get behind the ball whenever possible. The position of the glove and fingers should be emphasized here (Photo 6-3). Balls above the waist are caught with the fingers up; below the waist the fingers are in a down position. The use of one hand in catching the ball is seen more and more today, but we believe you should drill your players in the use of two hands. Tell them after they make the "pros" that they can use one hand. Teach them the following cues, all important in catching fly balls:

• Catch the ball while moving toward the target of your throw.

Photo 6-3

- Try to use as few steps as possible when throwing—this saves time.
- Catch the ball on the throwing side.
- Never run with glove hand extended when trying to catch an exceptionally long drive. Teach your players to turn and run at top speed to the spot where they think the ball will come down; turn and make the catch; or extend arms at the proper moment to catch ball.

Ground Balls. Get directly behind the ball whenever possible. The glove hand should be slightly off the center line of the outfielder's body and to the inside of the front foot (Photo 6-4). Remember, the front foot should be the foot on the glove side. Move into the ball—don't wait—if the ball has stopped, then bare-hand it. If there is no chance of the runner taking an extra base, block the ball with knee and body—remember, do not go down too soon (Photo 6-5). When a quick throw is necessary, move into the ball aggressively on a line with the target of the throw, like an infielder.

Photo 6-4

Photo 6-5

SPECIAL PLAYS OF THE OUTFIELDER

The Scoop Play

Control is the key to success in this play. The outfielder must charge the ball aggressively, but get the body *in control* by the time the ball is

Photo 6-6

approximately 15 to 20 feet from him. He should remember to maintain proper stride and as the ball nears, reach down and scoop ball up with glove hand (Photo 6-6), continue in stride straight up and make a strong overhand throw.

Throwing

Movement is important in achieving a good throw. Outfielders should be taught to move aggressively toward the target. The player should catch the ball, whenever possible, while he is in motion. This adds force to his throw if body mechanics are applied correctly. In catching the ball, the outfielder grasps it firmly *across* the *seams*, and uses the crow hop to maintain speed and help in lining up the direction of the throw. We teach the overhand throw because it is the best throw to use to get a true carry and bounce. The throw should be low (face high) to the cutoff man; this type of throw is easier to handle in case a change of direction is necessary. Drills dealing with throwing the ball face high and on glove side of a relay man assist in making the movement automatic for both the outfielder and the relay man. The follow-through must be complete.

Playing the Fence

An intelligent outfielder will inspect the outfield prior to all games and acquaint himself with the playing condition of the field. Is the grass high, or low; is the ground soft, or hard; are there bare patches, etc.? If a fence is involved, the outfielder should take a close look at its type and height, and notice whether there is a warning track and if it affords the fielder sufficient time for adjustment. You should work on individual speed and reaction time with each of your outfielders so that they become familiar with their ability to go to and off a fence. Drills dealing with the following are stressed as well: (a) Teammates verbally assisting each other as they approach the fence; (b) rebounds and caroms off a fence; (c) combinations of both of the above.

Playing the Sun Field

Playing a sun field requires that the outfielders learn how to use sunglasses; learn how to shade their eyes with glove hand or bare hand, and to change the angle from the sun. Having sunglasses available for the outfielders is a must. The glasses that require a slight tap are easy to adjust to fit all fielders; knowing the position of the sun prior to play will help the fielder in blocking it out with the glove or bare hand. Finally, drills showing fielders how to catch the ball on an angle from the sun will also be an asset.

PRIORITIES: WHO HAS THE RIGHT-OF-WAY?

The outfield should follow some very basic rules dealing with the right-of-way to the ball. In almost all situations, if these basics are followed, the chances for a properly completed play are increased tremendously. The rules are:

1. The center fielder takes anything he can reach *unless* wind direction dictates otherwise, or if another outfielder is in better position to throw.
2. The center fielder has priority over left fielder or right fielder.
3. All outfielders have priority over infielders.
4. Outfielders should call loudly and continually until they make the catch.
5. When one outfielder is making the catch, other outfielders should call his name to reassure him there is no danger of collision (fence or another fielder).
6. Each outfielder should always wait until he is sure he can catch the fly ball before he calls it (wait until it reaches its full height). See Illustration 6-1.

Center fielder (8) has priority over left fielder (7) and right fielder (9) and all infielders (5), (6), (4), (3).

Left fielder (7) and right fielder (9) have priority over all infielders (5), (6), (4), (3).

Shortstop (6) has priority over all other infielders (5), (4), (3).

Shortstop (6) and second baseman (4) have priority over third baseman (5) and first baseman (3).

Third baseman (5) and first baseman (3) have priority over catcher (2) and pitcher (1).

Catcher (2) takes anything that the third baseman (5) and first baseman (3) cannot reach.

Pitcher (1) is the last man on the totem pole. He takes anything no one can reach.

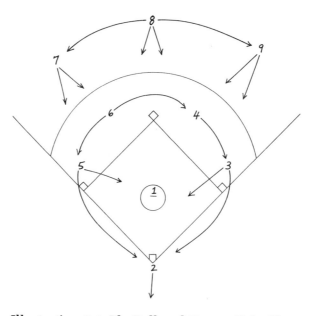

Illustration 6-1. Fly Ball and Pop-up Priorities

DRILLS TO DEVELOP
YOUR OUTFIELDERS' SKILLS

Charge, Scoop and Throw Drill

Purpose: To prevent runners from taking that extra base by practicing a rapid approach to a rolling or bouncing ball, quick fielding, quick release of the ball and a strong accurate throw.

Description: All outfielders line up in a single file at one outfield position, or outfielders assume their respective outfield positions (Illustration 6-2). From the pitcher's mound the ball is either thrown or batted to the receiving outfielder. The outfielder charges the ball at top speed, circling the ball so that he is heading not only toward the ball, but also the base he intends to throw to, scoops up the ball with his gloved hand and without destroying his momentum by stopping or turning, throws in an overhand fashion low and on one bounce to the base. If a cutoff man is available, the throw should be aimed at his head; the cutoff man should station himself so that he is of assistance to the outfielder in making an accurate throw and be the correct distance away from the intended base. If the throw is not cut off, the ball will take the proper length bounce.

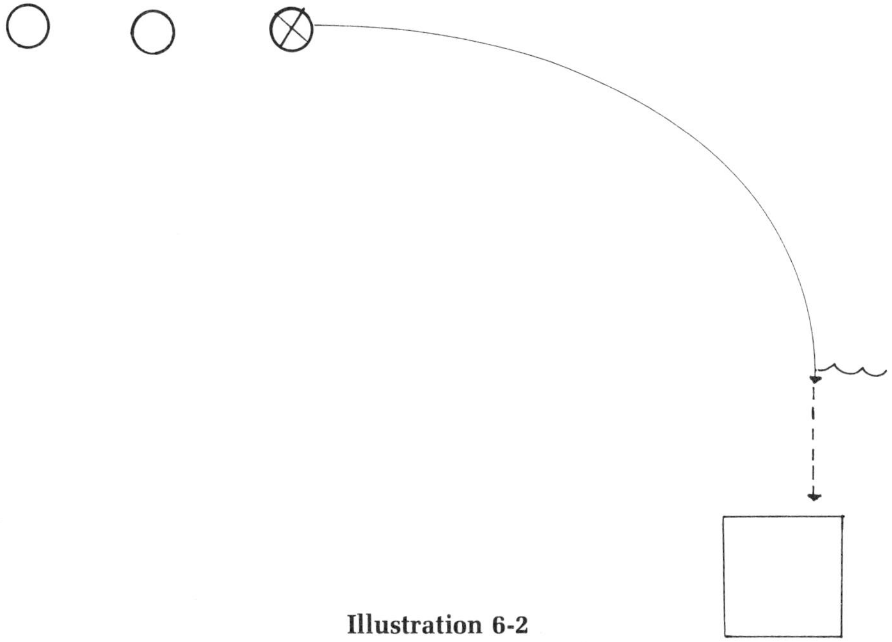

Illustration 6-2

Additional values: This is an active type of drill which may stimulate interest in practice sessions. The players develop confidence in their ability to field under pressure of speed and in turn this leads to the development of aggressive players.

To add to realism and purpose: A base runner may be added who will try to advance two bases from his base of origin as the ball is batted or thrown to the outfielder. Runners may attempt to go from home to second, first to third, or second to home. Runners should wear batting helmets and sliding pads.

Caution: This drill should not be used unless the players' throwing arms are in condition or unless the drill is modified to exclude or minimize the strain of throwing.

Sensational Catches

Purpose: To develop the skills required in turning and running after a ball hit to the fielder's left or right, in front of him or behind him.

Description: Outfielders line up in a single file. The first fielder in line takes a position about 150 feet in front of the second and throws the ball in any direction far enough away from the second fielder so that he will have to catch the ball while running at top speed. The thrower then returns to the end of the line and the person who has just fielded the ball becomes the thrower.

Fielding Response Drill

Purpose: To develop response speed.

Description:

1. When the ball is to fielder's left or right, the fielder pivots 90 degrees on the foot nearest to the line of flight of the ball and then takes a crossover step with his other foot. For quick attainment of maximum speed the first few steps should be short, choppy, and hard driving so that momentum is built up while proper body alignment is maintained and balance is not lost. The fielder runs at top speed even when he might have the time to glide over to the ball. See Illustration 6-3.

2. When the ball is behind the outfielder, the fielder pivots 180 degrees on the foot nearest to the line of the ball followed by a crossover step with his other foot. He runs directly to the spot where he has estimated the ball is to land and does not turn

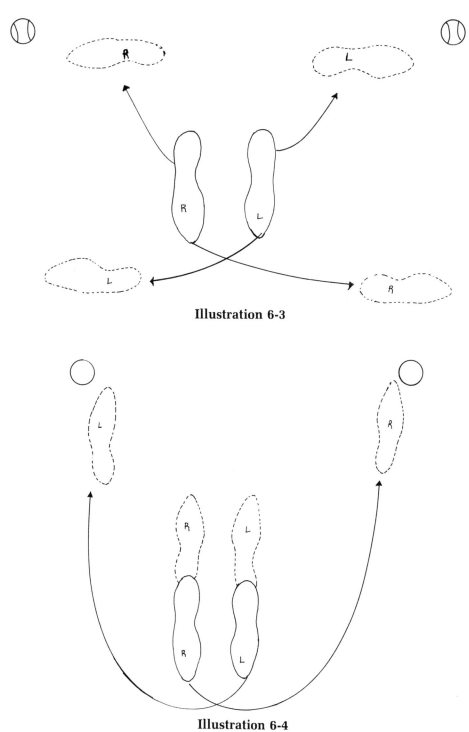

Illustration 6-3

Illustration 6-4

his head and look for the ball until he has reached this spot. See Illustration 6-4.

3. When the ball is in front of the fielder no pivot or crossover step is involved. He should run on the balls of the feet to minimize jarring the body and causing the ball to appear to bounce in flight. If time permits the fielder may practice circling the ball and timing his catch so that he is in the best possible position to throw to a given base.

Tag-up Throw

Purpose: To teach outfielder the skill of taking the proper step forward as he catches the ball as well as practice in throwing. (See Illustration 6-5 for drill setup.)

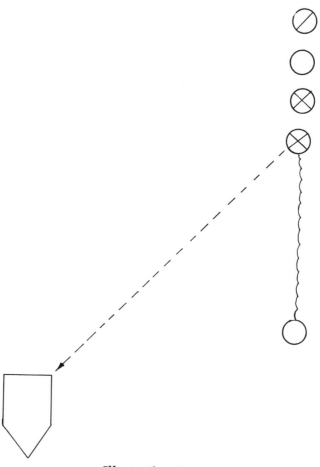

Illustration 6-5

Description: Place a runner on second or third base. Outfielder attempts to stand a step behind the ball (Illustration 6-6) so that if he throws with his right hand he will be stepping forward with his right foot as he catches the ball. This provides the necessary momentum and arm-leg coordination needed to make the throw strong and accurate without wasting time with additional steps.

Illustration 6-6

Bounce Ball

Purpose: To develop in outfielders the ability to throw low and on one bounce. To practice the technique of throwing overhand and of attaining the proper backspin for the desired bounce. This drill is a good early season conditioner for outfielders' throwing arms.

Description: The outfielders pair off and then face each other standing about 100 feet apart (Illustration 6-7). Each pair has a ball to bounce back and forth to each other attempting to achieve the longest bounce possible. The partners gradually keep moving farther apart until they are throwing at a distance of about 250 feet.

Illustration 6-7

Illustration 6-8

Rebound Relay

Purpose: To develop the skill of fielding a batted ball that has struck the fence (Illustration 6-8), then turning toward the gloved hand (Illustrations 6-9 and 6-10) and throwing approximately 150 feet to a relay man (Illustration 6-11) so that he receives the ball at head height without a bounce.

Description: Have the outfielders form in a single line. The first person in line steps forward and becomes the fielder. A coach or the second person in line throws the ball past the fielder up

Illustration 6-9

Illustration 6-10

against a fence. The play is made, then the second person in line becomes the fielder and the original fielder returns to the end of the line.

Caution: Do not work this complete drill unless throwing arms are in condition. Do not let any infielder or outfielder make too many throws unless there is ample rest in between. (Infielders sometimes have to field throws which get past them and strike a fence in foul territory.)

Illustration 6-11

Quick-Start Foot Drill

Purpose: To develop the ability for quick starts and movements in various directions.

Description: Outfielders stand in their normal stance, approximately 25 to 35 feet from each other or a coach, who throws a ball over their head and shoulder area. Have the outfielders turn to the right on balls tossed over their right shoulder; they turn to the left on balls tossed over their left shoulder.

Ground Ball Drills

No one on base

Purpose: To develop the ability to get to the ball and field it properly.

Description: When a ground ball is hit to the outfield (by coach), the outfielder will charge the ball until he gets 12 to 15 feet in front of the ball. The outfielder will go down on one knee on his throwing side, if the ball is rolling and not bouncing (no one on base). If the ball is bouncing, he should time it and field it with two hands as an infielder, then crow-hop as he throws. You, the coach, should remember to stress that right-handed players should go down on right knee, and left-handed fielders go down on their left knee.

Runners on base

Purpose: To develop the skill of being aggressive as an outfielder.

Description: Each fielder is taught to charge the ball aggressively until he is 12 to 15 feet from ball; at this point, he should be *under control.* * This can be accomplished by taking short choppy steps as he closes the distance between him and the ball. If the ball bounces true, use two hands to catch the ball and crow-hop and throw; if the ball is rolling, the outfielder should make a one-hand glove pick up on his glove side and to the outside of his foot, crow-hop and throw.

Infield Drill for the Outfield

Purpose: To develop the ability to field ground balls.

Description: Let outfielders position themselves in the infield. Ground balls are hit by the coaching staff. Instruction in proper techniques are reinforced by the staff as the outfielders catch the balls.

Outfield Drills: Playing the Ball in the Sun

Purpose: To develop the ability to play the ball in the sun.

Description: Position the outfielders and hit fungoes to them so that all balls will be directly in the sun for them.

Points to emphasize to outfielders:

1. keep the sun shielded from your eyes with your glove hand prior to the pitch.
2. if ball is hit, keep glove in this shielded position until you can position yourself for the catch without looking directly into the sun.

If using sunglasses, additional practice is necessary. Glasses are not flipped down until the outfielder knows exactly where the ball is.

---

*As a teaching cue, *under control* can be applied to many drills to help the learning process.

Indoor Drill for Outfielders

The object of this drill is to work on the proper mechanics for fielding fly balls and ground balls. Outfielders position themselves behind one another at the far end of the gym. The coach, and a player catching for him, are stationed at the other end of the gym. The coach begins the drill by rolling ground balls to each outfielder. The outfielder fields the ball while working on his footwork and body position. He also works on his scoop play by fielding the ball to the outside and in front of the stride foot. When he catches the ball he uses a crow-hop to get his body under control and get his momentum going forward for his throw. After rolling six or seven balls at the outfielder, the coach now begins to roll the ball to either side of the outfielder. This enables the fielder to work on his crossover or drop step to get the ball quickly.

The next part of the drill begins with the coach throwing a fly ball directly to each outfielder. The fielder fields the ball by catching it on his throwing side, and moves in on it. The outfielder throws the ball using good throwing mechanics to the fielder fielding for the coach as if he were a cutoff or relay man.

After six or seven throws directly to the outfielder, the coach now begins to throw the ball to the left and right of the outfielder. The outfielder works on his crossover step to get a good jump on the ball, catches it, and throws it in.

The outfielders now move into the center of the gym and assume their normal stance. The coach throws fly balls over the outfielder's head so he can work on his drop step to open his body toward the ball. The fielder catches the ball and throws it in as quickly as possible.

TIPS FOR OUTFIELDERS

1. Practice catching fly balls and ground balls.
2. Outfielders should run in and out to their respective positions.
3. Back up bases and, if necessary, cover an open base.
4. Use your voice to help and communicate with other outfielders and infielders.
5. Throw overhand, never sidearm.

6. Assume the strength of right-handed hitters is toward left field.

7. Assume the strength of left-handed hitters is toward right field.

8. Play deep for big men or players who swing extremely hard.

9. Play shallow on small men or players who choke up on the bat.

10. Watch the opposing team during batting practice. See who hits the ball hard and to what part of the field.

11. Use the crossover step.

12. Hit the cutoff or relay man.

13. Know when *not* to catch a foul fly ball.

14. Learn to wear sunglasses.

TEAM DEFENSE:
Philosophy and Drills

7

Every team must develop a plan for defense to be an effective unit in the field. Practices should always be run with drills that have a purpose and the coach wants to discover what are the successful ways to stop opponents from scoring. This controlled situation practice is important, for you will discover that nothing can be taken for granted. Nothing can be automatic because too many factors or even just one factor can cause the need for an adjustment by the team. Such factors can be the absence of a player, a weak arm, or even the score and inning. Any of these factors may *force* you to defense a play in a different manner.

Where do you start with "Team Defense"? We believe it starts with the word "attitude." Nobody will ever catch the ball if he does not want to. To go even a step further, your whole team must want to play defense in order to be successful at it. Let's not forget that human beings play the game of baseball, and therefore, we will always have errors of commission and omission, but we want to keep them to a limited number. Confidence, as displayed by the entire team in aggressively attacking the ball on defense, will also be a positive factor in developing defensive attitude. Team defense is the direct outgrowth of every player being involved in playing a ball.

Movement and verbal communication on the part of the entire team is necessary whenever a ball is hit. A ball to the left side causes the shortstop and third baseman to try to catch it; the second baseman and right fielder move to back up first base in case of a poor throw; the left fielder and center fielder charge in, anticipating that the ball may take a bad bounce or be played poorly. The catcher backs up first base if the situation warrants it, and the pitcher prepares to assist if he is needed. Every player on the field is involved and performing a task to complete a play. Their movements may not be needed that time, but we all know that it is when someone fails to do his task that the play is a poor one and perhaps causes the game to be lost.

You should also drill your team in knowing the game situation. How often do you see a player catch a ball and then forget what he should be doing with it? Hesitation on the part of the defense allows the other team to remain on the attack. Every player on the field must know what he is going to do with the ball if it should come his way. Will he go for a force out? a double play? getting the runner at the plate? Every player must anticipate every possible defensive situation, and work on the ability to handle his assignment. If your coach knows your players' range and ability, you will know what to expect from your players. If a player does not have the ability to complete a play, then it is your responsibility to assist him and the team. This assistance can be in terms of cutoffs, relays, or substitutions.

Before reviewing different team situations, look over the following list of basics—they will help you to instill good team attitude and confidence, but only if you work at them. Remember, no one can expect players to read a list and then be able to perform each task. You, as a coach, must work with them in developing the physical and mental skills that are necessary for good individual and team defense.

TEAM DEFENSE: THE BASICS

1. Always want and anticipate that every ball will be hit to you.
2. Always be in the proper ready stance for your position in the field.
3. Know what you will do with the ball before it is hit to you.
4. Always play the ball; don't let it play you.
5. Know the playing field: the fence, the grass, the skin part of the field. This will remind you to keep low, and anticipate the bad hop that always comes up at your throat.
6. Know who should be covering a base in a particular situation, and remind each other who should cover.
7. Use the scoop play only when necessary.
8. Watch the ball and catch it first. We have never seen a play completed without the ball first being caught.

9. Know your pitcher's ability and pitches.

10. Know and study your opponents at bat.

11. Know the sun and wind conditions on the field.

12. Be aware of priorities on fly balls.

13. Let each other know that the field is clear for them to catch a fly ball.

14. Always run on and off the field.

15. Know the basics for your position and add them to this list.

DEFENSIVE CUTOFF AND RELAY PRINCIPLES

1. Whenever possible, bases should be covered where there is a possibility of a play.

2. The cutoff man must think quickly and anticipate the play instantly. He must know beforehand which runner is the important one to put out. You, the coach, must alert your team prior to the pitch as to what you wish them to do. When the game is on the line, you must take the responsibility and inform the team of your decision. The entire team must be well drilled in the movements that are required and all throws toward the cutoff man should be *low enough* for him to handle.

3. Communication is important, not only between the cutoff man and the player covering the base, but especially among the outfielders on all plays when a ball is hit between them or over their heads.

4. Infielders should not interfere with the base runners, but should position themselves inside the base. This tends to make the runner take a wider turn at the base. The infielders should watch the runners to be sure they really tag the base. Many outs are recorded by this heads-up procedure.

5. Whenever possible, the outfielders should practice strong, low hard throws to second base. This can occur on all routine fly balls to the outfield with no one on base. This practice will prepare the fielder to develop good habits so that he will be ready when it counts.

6. Practice will help to overcome weaknesses, but remember, "Perfect Practice Makes Perfect."

7. Here are some common words used in communication:

Cut—   Cut this throw and be ready to throw to another base.
Nothing—Let this throw go through.
Relay—   Cut the throw and relay the ball to the man calling "relay."

THE TANDEM OR PIGGYBACK RELAY

This is used by the shortstop and second baseman on a batted ball that is a sure double or a possible triple. On a batted ball to left field, left-center field or center field, the shortshop should be the lead man. On a batted ball to right center field or right field, the second baseman should be the lead man. You can change this procedure and let the player with the stronger arm always be the lead man.

The lead man should sprint into the outfield in the direction of the batted ball. He should have his right hand raised straight above his head and his glove hand outstretched parallel to the ground. When the outfielder retrieves the ball, turns and looks for the relay man, he sees the relay man in this position and he has a target to throw at. The outfield should throw the ball to the relay man's glove side. As the ball is coming toward the relay man, he should turn toward his glove side and start drifting toward the infield. As he receives the ball he should have his momentum going in the direction he wants to throw and gets rid of the ball as quickly as possible.

The back man positions himself 15 to 20 feet behind the lead man. The back man has the responsibility of lining up the lead man and telling him where he is to throw the ball. He is also there to back up the lead man in case of an errant throw by the outfielder. If the throw is over the lead man's head or if he has to jump to catch it, he should let it go. The back man should be in position so he can catch the ball on a fly or one bounce. Then he makes the throw to the infield. If the throw to the lead man is a short hop or an in-between hop, the lead man should step out of the way and let the ball go to the back man. He will then make the throw to the infield.

Team defense is most apparent and involved when it comes to defensing the sacrifice bunt. Regardless of what method you use, the main emphasis is on doing it properly. The defense is set up to get the lead runner and all drills and practices are designed to meet this task. Perfect practice makes perfect and in defensing the bunt this means *get an out!*

If you can't get the lead runner, get the next possible out somewhere. As all coaches will say, "GET *SOMEBODY!*"

SAMPLE TEAM DEFENSIVE SITUATIONS

This section shows sample game situations with emphasis on two major defensive areas: cutoff and relays, and defensive assignments on bunt situations.

We begin with a typical game situation, such as a single to left field with no runners on base. We then list each player and explain each of their jobs in relation to the rest of the team. To further help you visualize the hypothetical scene, each situation is fully illustrated with a diagram.

You may want to adapt these sample game situations into your own practices. They provide practical, detailed examples of working together defensively as a team.

CUTOFF AND RELAYS

Situation:

Single to left field, no one on base (part one)

Pitcher (1)	Takes a position halfway between mound and second base (nose for ball).
Catcher (2)	Remains at home base.
First baseman (3)	Observes the runner tagging the base when he makes his turn and covers the base.
Shortstop (6)	Takes throw from left field at second base.
Second baseman (4)	Backs up the shortstop at second base.
Third baseman (5)	Observes activity—protects third base area—be ready in case of poor throw.
Center fielder (8)	Backs up left fielder.
Right fielder (9)	Advances in toward first base area—lining up with throw from left fielder—in case of poor throw.
Left fielder (7)	Throws strong low throw to second base.

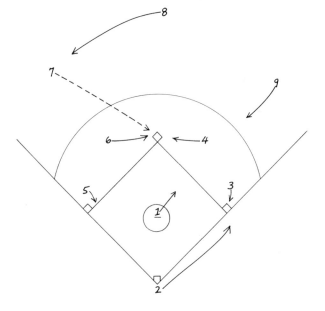

Situation:

Single to left field, no one on base (part two)

Note: The difference between the first and second situation is where the shortstop goes out to the cutoff position. All other actions by players are basically the same. Observe the movement of the second baseman (4) and the first baseman (3).

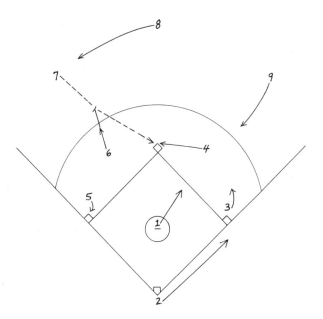

Situation:

Single to left field, man on first base

Player:

(1) Moves to back up third base.
(2) Remains at home plate to protect against a runner scoring.
(3) Covers first base.
(4) Covers second base.
(5) Covers third base.
(6) Becomes the cutoff man on the throw from the left fielder to third base.
(7) Makes a low strong throw through cutoff man to third base.
(8) Moves to back up left fielder.
(9) Moves toward the infield to assist if necessary.

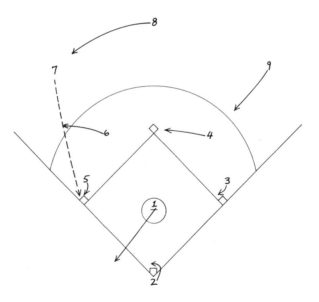

Situation:

*Single to left field, runner on second
or runners on first and third*

Player:

(1) Moves halfway between third and home and observes the play as it develops.
(2) Remains at home plate for possible play.
(3) Covers first base and observes play development.
(4) Covers second base and observes play development.
(5) Assumes the role of cutoff man between left fielder and home.
(6) Covers third base and observes play development.
(7) Charges the ball while under control and makes strong, low throw through cutoff man to home plate.
(8) Backs up left fielder and offers communication as to play development.
(9) Moves toward second base area.

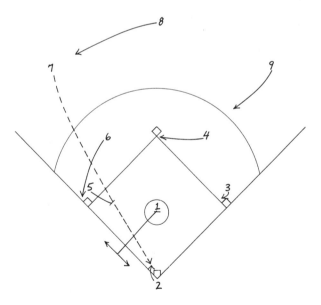

Situation:

Single to left field between third and short,
runners on second or second and third bases

Player:

(1)   Backs up home plate.
(2)   Covers home plate.
(3)   Stays near first base.
(4)   Covers second base.
(5)   Cutoff man to home plate.
(6)   Covers third.
(7)   Makes strong low throw to home plate.
(8)   Moves to back up left fielder.
(9)   Comes in to assist and possibly cover first base, if necessary.

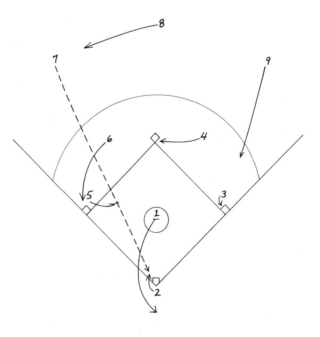

Situation:

Double, possible triple, to left center with runners on third and second or both third and second with no one on base

Player:

(1) Halfway between third and home and watches play develop.

(2) Remains at home.

(3) Follows or trails the batter (runner) to second base, covers the bag in case a play develops if runner rounds base too far.

(4) Becomes the second man or backup man in the "double relay"—trails the shortstop approximately 30 feet behind him while in line with third base.*

(5) Covers third base and positions himself on left side of base.

(6) Is the main or premier relay man. Goes out to left field to get throw from outfielder—first or head man in "double relay."

(7) Makes low hard throw to shortstop. Does not try to throw to third base.

(8) Backs up left fielder or makes throw as above if he gets to ball first.

(9) Comes in to back up second base.

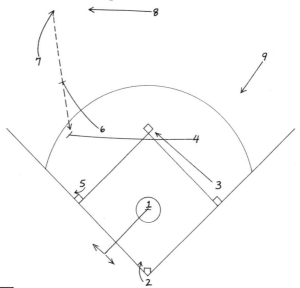

*Double relay is used for two purposes:

    a. To back the first relay man in case of bad throw.

    b. To tell the first relay man what to do when he receives the ball from the outfielder. This is sometimes referred to as a "piggyback relay."

Situation:

Double, maybe triple, to left center, runners on first, first and second or perhaps loaded bases

Player:

(1) Must be prepared to watch play develop. Goes halfway between third and home and then backs up the base where the play develops.

(2) Stays at home plate.

(3) Trails runner to second base and then is the cutoff man from the double relay group.

(4) Is the second man of the "double relay." About 30 feet behind the shortstop—in line with throw from outfield to either third or home—alerts shortstop as to possible play.

(5) Covers third base—stands on left side of base.

(6) Goes to get first throw from left fielder—relay man #1.

(7) Makes strong throw to shortstop.

(8) Backs up left fielder.

(9) Moves toward the infield to assist if necessary.

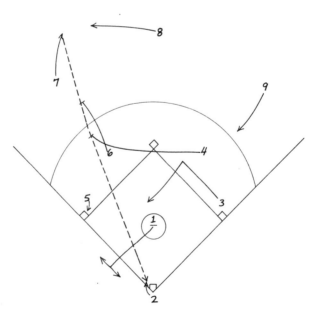

Situation:

Double, maybe triple, down left field foul line, man on first base

Player:

(1) Watches play develop—halfway between home and third.
(2) Remains to cover home plate.
(3) Follows runner toward second base and becomes cutoff man if needed.
(4) Is the second part of the double relay (trailer) behind the shortstop.
(5) Covers third base.
(6) Relay man #1.
(7) Makes strong throw to shortstop.
(8) Backs up the left fielder.
(9) Covers toward infield (right side).

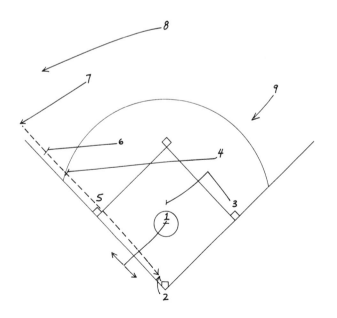

Situation:

No runners on base, single to center field

Player:

(1) Observes play and moves to position halfway between mound and second base.

(2) Remains at home plate.

(3) Makes sure runner tags first base when making the turn, and remains at first to protect in case of a rundown.

(4) Watches throw from center and backs up throw to shortstop covering second.

(5) Remains at third.

(6) Covers center fielder's throw to second base.

(7) Rounds behind center fielder and communicates with him.

(8) Makes strong low throw to second base.

(9) Same as left fielder.

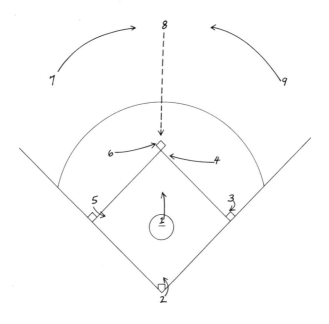

Situation:

Runner on first, single to center field

Player:

(1) Moves to back up third base.
(2) Remains at home plate.
(3) Covers first base.
(4) Covers second base.
(5) Remains at third— covers base.
(6) Is the cutoff man between center fielder and third base.
(7) Left fielder moves toward third base in foul ground.
(8) Makes strong, hard, low throw to third base.
(9) Backs up center fielder.

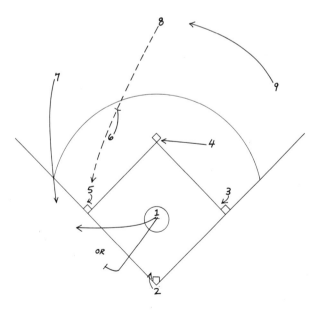

Situation:

Single to center field, runner on second base, or runners on second and third bases

Player:

(1) Moves to back up home plate.

(2) Protects home plate.

(3) Must move to cutoff position.

(4) Attempts to field ball and moves to assist by verbal communication.

(5) Remains at third for possible play.

(6) Attempts to field ball, then must cover second base.

(7) Backs up center fielder—communication is essential!

(8) Makes strong, low throw to plate, over the cutoff man's head, but within fielding area.

(9) Backs up center fielder—communication is essential!

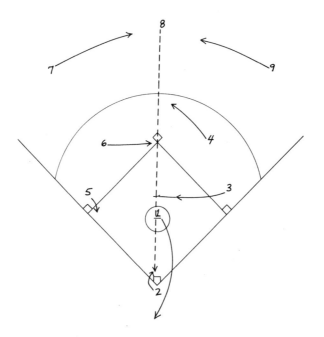

Situation:

Single to center, runners on first and second or bases full

Player:

(1) Takes position halfway between home plate and third. Will back up base where the play develops. Must observe action and throw.

(2) Protects home plate.

(3) Reacts to be cutoff man to home plate.

(4) Covers second base.

(5) Covers third base.

(6) Observes action and becomes a possible cutoff man with the throw to third base.

(7) Backs up center fielder.

(8) Makes a hard throw through either cutoff man. He reacts to what he sees and to what he hears from his teammates.

(9) Moves in to infield.

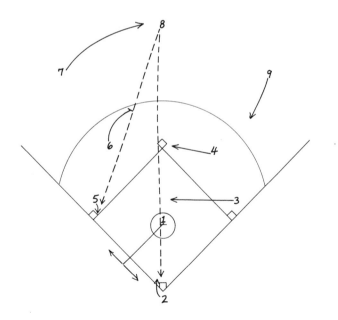

Situation:

Fly ball to right or center field, runners on first and third, or bases loaded

Player:

(1)   Moves to back up home plate.

(2)   Remains at home to protect it.

(3)   Becomes the cutoff man in either case.

(4)   Moves to cover first base.

(5)   Protects third base.

(6)   Covers second base.

(7)   Moves into infield.

(8) (9)   Moves toward fly ball or if fielding ball, makes strong throw through the cutoff man to plate. (Direction of throw will depend on distance of fly ball, score, etc.)

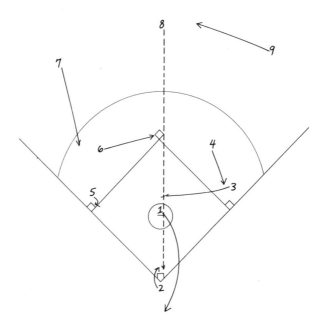

Situation:

Bases empty, single to right field

Player:

(1) Goes to a position halfway between mound and second base.

(2) Remains at home.

(3) Observes that the runner tags first base while making the turn. Stays to cover first base.

(4) Covers second base. Takes throw from right fielder.

(5) Remains to protect third base area.

(6) Backs up right fielder's throw to second base.

(7) Moves in toward third base.

(8) Backs up right fielder.

(9) Makes low, strong throw to second base.

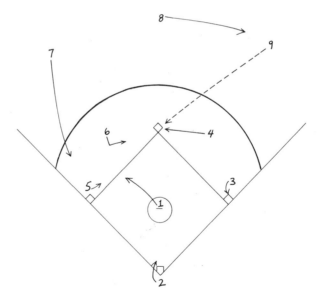

Situation:

Single to right field, runner on first base, or runners on first and third

Player:

(1) Moves to back up third base—lines up with throw.

(2) Remains to protect home plate.

(3) Remains to cover first base and observes runner tag base.

(4) Remains to cover second base—observes runner tagging second base.

(5) Covers third base.

(6) Becomes the cutoff man between right fielder and third base.

(7) Moves in toward third base.

(8) Backs up right fielder.

(9) Makes strong low throw through cutoff man to third base.

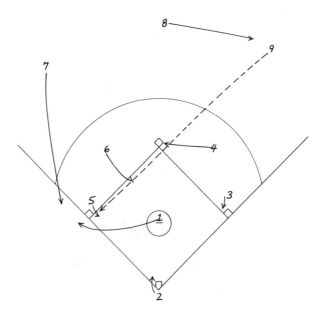

Situation:

Single to right field, runners on second base or runners on second and third bases

Player:

(1) Moves to back up home plate.
(2) Protects home plate.
(3) Becomes the cutoff man between right field and home plate. Takes position about 45 feet from home plate.
(4) Moves to cover first base.
(5) Protects third base—possible cut—third play.
(6) Protects second base—possible cut—second play.
(7) Moves in toward third base.
(8) Backs up right fielder.
(9) Makes strong throw through cutoff man to plate.

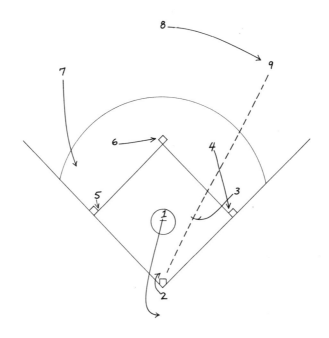

Situation:

> *Runners on first and second or bases full, single to right field*

Player:

(1) Assumes position halfway between third and home—reacts to play.

(2) Protects home plate.

(3) Will be the cutoff man if throw is made to plate.

(4) Covers second base.

(5) Covers third base.

(6) Will be the cutoff man for throw to third base.

(7) Moves in to assist; backs up third base.

(8) Backs up right fielder.

(9) Can do one of many things. All will depend on score and number of outs. Some basics to observe: Never allow tying or winning run from going to third with less than two outs. Give up the runs to keep tying run at second. Don't make the foolish throw.

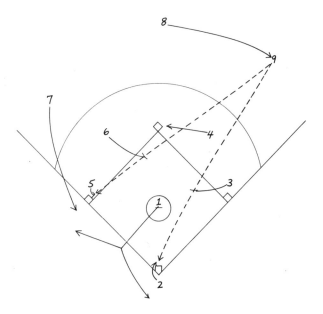

Situation:

No one on base, man on third base or second; or man on third and second bases, double, possible triple, to right-center field

Player:

(1) Backs up third, gets deep.

(2) Protects home plate.

(3) Trails the runner (original batter) to second base; covers bag for possible play at that base.

(4) Goes out to center field, lines up between third base and fielder of ball. He is the relay man.

(5) Covers third base.

(6) Becomes the trail about 30 feet behind the second baseman. Lines up with third base.

(7) Moves in toward third base.

(8) Gets to ball and makes strong throw to relay man.

(9) Backs up center fielder.

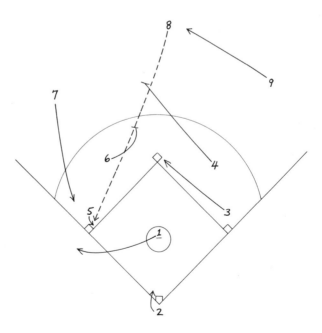

Situation:

Double, possible triple, to right-center field—man on first base, or man on first and second bases, or bases loaded

Player:

(1)   Goes halfway between third and home, sees where the throw is coming, and then backs up the proper base.

(2)   Covers home plate.

(3)   Trails runner and moves to middle of diamond for cutoff.

(4)   Is the cutoff man.

(5)   Covers third base.

(6)   Trails the relay man.

(7)   Moves into area behind third base.

(8) (9) Goes after the ball and make strong throw to relay man, who in turn throws to third or home.

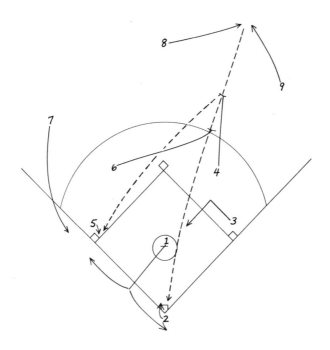

Situation:

No one on bases; double, possible triple down right field line

Player:

(1)   Backs up third base.

(2)   Protects home plate.

(3)   Trails runner to second base—possible tag play.

(4)   Becomes the first relay man (double relay).

(5)   Covers third base.

(6)   Is the trailer relay man (double relay).

(7)   Moves into area behind third base.

(8)   Backs up right fielder.

(9)   Makes strong throw to first relay man.

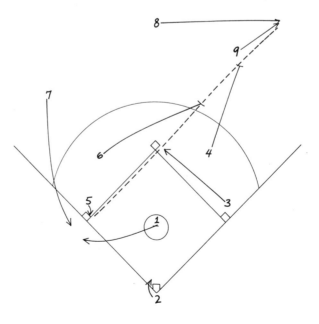

Situation:

Man on first base, triple, possible home run down right field line

Player:

(1) Goes halfway between home and third—sees where throw is going—reacts to play.

(2) Covers home plate.

(3) Trails second baseman and remains 30 feet behind.

(4) Relay man—goes into right field—lines up between right fielder and home. Distance out is determined by where right fielder fields ball.

(5) Covers third base.

(6) Is cutoff man.

(7) Moves in toward third base.

(8) Backs up right fielder.

(9) Makes strong throw to relay man.

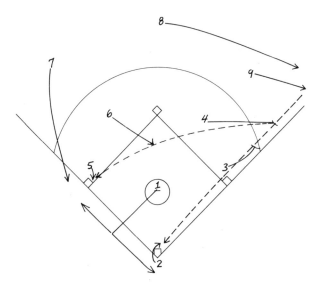

DEFENSIVE ASSIGNMENTS ON BUNT SITUATIONS

Situation:

With a runner on first base

Player:

(1) Breaks toward home plate after delivering the ball.
(2) Fields all bunts possible; calls the play; covers third base when third baseman fields the bunt in close to home plate.
(3) Covers the area between first base and the pitcher's mound.
(4) Covers first base . . . cheats by shortening position.
(5) Covers the area between third and the pitcher's mound.
(6) Covers second base.
(7) Moves in toward second base area.
(8) Backs up second base.
(9) Backs up second base.

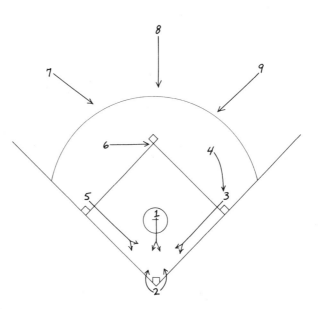

Situation:

With runners on first and second

Player:

(1)   Breaks toward the third base line upon delivering the ball.

(2)   Fields bunts in front of home plate; *calls the play*.

(3)   Is responsible for all balls in the area between first base and in a direct line from the mound to home plate.

(4)   Covers first base.

(5)   Takes a position on the edge of the grass; calls the play—whether the pitcher or the third baseman is to field the bunt.

(6)   Holds runner close to the base before the pitch; covers second base.

(7)   Backs up third base.

(8)   Backs up second base.

(9)   Backs up first base. Note: First objective is to retire the runner at third base, but one runner *must* be retired.

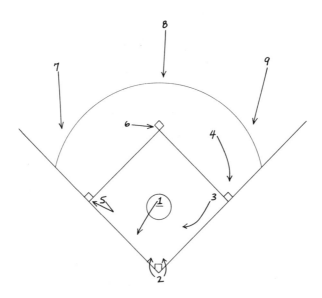

Situation:

With runners on first and second

Player:

(1) Breaks toward the plate.

(2) Catcher fields bunts in front of plate or *calls the play*.

(3) Charges toward the plate.

(4) Covers first base.

(5) Charges toward the plate.

(6) Bluffs runner back to second then races to cover third.

(7) Backs up third base.

(8) Backs up second base.

(9) Backs up first base.

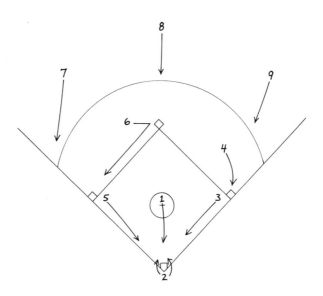

PLANNING AGAINST THE STEAL:
THE RUNDOWN PLAY

Every team must have a planned defense against a rundown situation. Two basic systems used are the rotating and one-throw rundown defense.

The Rotating Rundown System

Rundown between first and second bases

When a runner is caught off first base the pitcher immediately breaks toward first and positions himself behind the base. The shortstop runs to cover second base and the second baseman runs toward first base to get behind the runner. The first baseman runs the runner about halfway to second base and throws the ball to the shortstop. After he throws the ball he continues toward second base by rotating to the right side of the runner. The shortstop receives the throw and runs toward first base as hard as he can. This is to get the runner going back toward the base at full speed. As the runner gets within a few feet of the second baseman the shortstop throws the ball to him. Since the runner is going full speed toward first base it will be impossible for him to stop and start in the opposite direction before being tagged out. The second baseman receives the throw and makes the tag. If the tag is not made, the shortstop continues toward first base in order to be in position if the rundown continues. As the rundown develops, the center fielder moves in on a direct line of the play about 15 feet behind second base in order to back up the play. The pitcher should not get involved in the rundown play unless he has to. He just backs up the other players or bases in case of any bad throws.

Rundown between second and third bases

As soon as the runner is caught off second base the pitcher breaks toward third and positions himself behind the base. The second baseman or shortstop, depending on who has the ball, runs the base runner about halfway to third base and throws the ball to the third baseman. After he throws the ball to third base he continues on to third base by rotating to the right side.

The third baseman runs the runner toward second base as hard as he can. As the runner gets a few feet from the fielder covering second base he makes his throw. The fielder receives the throw, steps up, and makes the tag. The third baseman continues toward second base after he throws the ball by keeping to the right side of the runner in case the rundown continues. If the second baseman started the rundown, the shortstop will be at second base to receive the throw from the third baseman. If the shortstop started the rundown, the second baseman will be covering second base. As the play develops the center fielder positions himself in line with the play and about 15 feet behind second base to back up any bad throws.

Rundown between third base and home plate

As soon as the runner is caught off third base, the pitcher breaks toward home plate, unless the play originates where the pitcher has the ball hit back at him on the ground. In this case, he runs toward the runner. The shortstop goes behind third base and the first baseman comes toward home plate. The third baseman runs the runner about halfway to home plate and then throws to the catcher. The catcher runs the runner back as hard as he can, and when the runner is a few feet from the shortstop, he throws the ball. The shortstop receives the throw and moves up to make the tag. Again, the rotation system is followed where you always rotate to the base to which you throw. When the rundown originates the left fielder moves down the line and backs up any bad throws.

If at any time a rundown starts with the pitcher having the ball and the runner is well off the base, the pitcher runs right at the runner, forcing the runner to commit himself first. The pitcher will throw to the base that the runner has committed himself to, and then will follow the procedure as outlined previously.

Note: The infielders should always be aware that the runner should be run back to the base where he started, so if an error is made he will not advance to the next base.

The One-Throw Rundown

At St. John's the philosophy is to complete the rundown play with one throw. We feel that by making only one throw there is less chance of error and the play can be completed quickly.

When a rundown situation occurs the infielder who has the ball immediately runs at full speed toward the runner. The object is to get the base runner moving at full speed toward the tagger or next base. The infielder, running toward the base runner, should be holding the ball at shoulder level in throwing position. This is so the tagger has sight of the ball at all times. The infielder with the ball runs on the outside of the base runner's right shoulder if he is a right-handed thrower, or outside the left shoulder if he is a left-handed thrower. This will avoid the ball being hidden by the runner's body. The tagger receiving the ball closes the distance between the runner and the other infielder by moving toward the runner. When the tagger sees that the runner is coming toward him at full speed, he gives a verbal signal and takes a step up to receive the ball. When the infielder with the ball hears the tagger's signal, he uses a dart-type throw, aiming chest high. The tagger receives the ball and makes the tag.

The tagger must be aware that the runner should not be too close to him when the throw is made. This can result in the runner passing him or forcing him to catch the ball and trying to tag the runner at the same time. The tagger must also make sure he does not get the ball too soon, allowing the runner to stop and retreat without being able to catch him. The right timing for the rundown is to tag the runner before he can stop and get into a controlled run. In case a mistake occurs during the rundown, there is always someone backing up the players involved.

DEFENSING THE FIRST AND THIRD DOUBLE STEAL

The first and third double steal can be an effective offensive weapon. Many coaches feel that if they can force the defensive team to make two long throws, it will increase the chances for the runner at third to score. A well-organized practice should coordinate the various play options and individual skills used to defense the double steal. The rundown used for the first and third double steal varies from the rundown used when only one runner is involved.

There are six major situations where the first and third double steal can be used:

1. The runner at first breaks toward second base as the pitcher releases the ball toward home (straight steal).

2. The runner at first breaks toward second base during the pitcher's delivery (early break).

3. The runner at first breaks toward second when the catcher receives the ball or is ready to throw the ball back to the pitcher (delayed steal).

4. The runner at first base tags up on an infield pop-up behind the first or third base foul lines.

5. The runner at first base tags up on a foul pop-up to the catcher deep behind home plate.

6. The runner at first base intentionally tries to get picked off first base.

When determining the defense you want to use, the following must be considered: the strength and weakness of the catcher's and infielder's arm; the speed of the baserunners, the score and game situation.

Defensing the Straight Steal

The runner on first base breaks toward second base as the pitcher delivers toward home. The runner either goes straight into second base or stops three-quarters of the way down and gets into a rundown. The runner on third base waits for the catcher's throw to pass the pitcher and breaks toward home.

To defense this, the catcher quickly looks at the runner on third base. If the runner is too far off the base, he throws to the third baseman. If the catcher throws to second base, the infielder covering the base is up in front ready to tag the runner or throw home. If a rundown situation occurs, the infielder who takes the throw either walks or uses a controlled run at the runner coming from first base. This allows him to watch both runners and set himself for a quick strong throw home. The first baseman moves up to get closer to the runner so a quick tag can be made.

There are other options that can be used to defense this situation:

- The catcher can throw the ball back to the pitcher, hoping to catch the runner at third base leaving too soon.

- The shortstop covers second base and the second baseman moves into a cutoff position between the pitcher and second base. The second baseman watches the runner at third base. If the runner breaks toward home he cuts the ball off and throws home. If the runner at third base stays, he lets the ball go through to the shortstop, who tags the runner.

- The catcher can throw the ball to the shortstop who moves up into the infield grass.

- The catcher throws the ball directly to third base.

Defensing the Early Break

The runner at first base breaks toward second base during the pitcher's stretch delivery. The runner is trying to get the pitcher to balk or throw to first base. If the pitcher throws to second base, the runner stops and gets into a rundown.

To defense this situation the pitcher steps back off the rubber. He looks at the runner at third base to freeze him or catch him leaving too early. If the runner at third base does not leave, the pitcher throws to the second baseman. The second baseman handles the rundown as explained in "Defensing the Straight Steal."

Defensing the Delayed Steal

The runner at first base uses a delayed steal to try and catch the middle infielders flat-footed. The runner at first base leaves just as the catcher is ready to throw the ball back to the pitcher.

To defense this situation the second baseman or shortstop moves in front of second base any time the catcher receives the ball. The catcher must always be aware that the runner can break toward second base. He must be ready to throw quickly back to the pitcher or to second base if the runner at first base breaks.

Defensing Foul Pop-ups to Infielders

A foul ball pop-up is hit behind first base or third base. The second baseman and first baseman or shortstop and third baseman go for the ball. As the ball is caught, the runner on first base tags up and goes to second base. The runner on third base tags up and waits for the throw. If the ball is thrown to second base, the runner at third base attempts to score.

To defense this situation there must be a cutoff man to shorten the throws. If the ball is hit down the first base line, the shortstop positions himself between first and second base. The infielder catching the ball immediately throws the ball to the shortstop. If the runner stays at third base, the shortstop either tags the runner leaving from first base or walks him back. If the runner at third base attempts to score, the shortstop throws home.

If the ball is hit down the third base line, the pitcher runs between third base and home. The infielder who catches the ball immediately throws the ball to the pitcher. The pitcher checks the third base runner and throws to second base to get the runner who tagged up from first base.

Defensing Foul Pop-ups to Catchers

A foul pop-up is hit deep behind the catcher. The runner at first base waits for the catcher to field the ball and tags up. The runner on third base tags and waits for the catcher to throw to second base. If the throw goes through to second base, the runner on third base comes home.

To defense this situation the shortstop runs to a cutoff position in front of the pitcher's mound. The catcher immediately throws the ball to the shortstop. The shortstop checks the runner at third base and throws to second base.

Defensing the Intentional Pickoff at First

The runner on first base takes a large lead to be picked off intentionally. When the pitcher makes a move to throw to first base, the runner sprints toward second base. When the first baseman throws to second base, the runner on third base breaks toward home.

To defense this situation a right-handed pitcher lifts his lead leg and steps toward third base. This will freeze the runner or pick him off if he is too far off the base.

If the runner on third is not breaking toward home, the pitcher turns and throws to either first or second base. A left-handed pitcher quickly steps back off the rubber and makes a quick throw to first base.

The primary objective in defensing any first and third double steal is not to let the runner at third score. The secondary objective is to get the out involving the runner at first base.

SMART AND AGGRESSIVE BASERUNNING:
Fundamental Techniques for Players and Coaches

8

The most undercoached and least understood phase of baseball (on all levels) is baserunning. Although it is important, foot speed is not the only attribute necessary to be an outstanding base runner. Other things that enter into the picture are craftiness, agility, reaction time, baseball sense, confidence, and daring.

A baseball team that is well schooled in the fundamentals of baserunning is a team that puts pressure on the opposing players to the point that it forces them to make mistakes. A daring and aggressive team on the bases is one that is thrilling to watch and a joy to coach. It should be your objective to make your runners aggressive on the bases, to put the pressure on and "screw it down" until your opponent, because of anxiety, makes a mistake that will allow you to take the extra base and eventually score the winning run. The ability to be a good base runner is something that can be taught to a great degree. It should be your aim to work at baserunning until your players can react to given situations almost instantaneously. This importance placed on baserunning must be stressed through long hours of drills and practice.

Field conditions (wet, lumpy grass in the outfield, wide open fields, astroturf, etc.) can cause the defensive team to play defensively. By being aggressive on the bases, you can force the opposing players into doing something that they are not used to doing, that is rushing after the ball to get it back to the infield quickly, exposing them to potential mistakes. Whenever a mistake is made, the aggressive base runner will be ready to take the extra base.

Your own attitude as the coach will largely determine how aggressive your runners will be. Your attitude must always be aggressive, constantly encouraging your runners to try to take any extra base they can get. If a runner, using good judgment, attempts to take the extra base and is thrown out because of an outstanding play by the defensive team, don't chew him out. Chewing him out may keep him from being as aggressive as he should be the next time he is on base. The runner should be encouraged even when he is thrown out. If the runner used poor judgment and is thrown out, then it is your job to explain why the judgment was poor so that he can correct it. This can be accomplished by using the baserunning drills described in this chapter.

WHERE GOOD BASERUNNING BEGINS

Baserunning begins in the dugout. Before the game your players should be observing members of the other team in their pregame drills. Your players should be checking the infielders and outfielders as to whether they are right or left-handed, their speed and quickness, arm strength and accuracy. Your players should pay close attention to the catcher on the opposing team. They should be looking for quickness of release, arm strength, accuracy, and from where he throws. Is he throwing from the catcher's box behind home plate, or is he throwing from in front of home plate? They should also watch each pitcher when he is warming up, to see if he has any flaws in his delivery that will give the runner any advantages. Does the pitcher have a high leg kick, break the hands slowly, etc.?

The instant your batter-runner has made contact with the ball, he must concern himself with getting out of the batter's box as quickly as possible. After the swing, he must gain his balance and head directly toward first base. In leaving the batter's box, the runner should take his first step with the back foot directly toward first base. This is the same for both the right and left-handed hitter. The runner should observe good running form, the body leaning slightly forward, and the arms pumping naturally forward and backward. You do not want him to pump his arms side to side because this will divert his momentum away from first base. The runner should be looking at the base, not at the ball.

The runner should touch the base with the ball of the foot on the top front portion of the base (Photo 8-1), using *either foot*. You do not

Photo 8-1

want to break stride or take baby steps in order to touch the base with either the right or left foot. The runner should run through the base at top speed. He should think of the base as a sprinter thinks of the tape at the finish line at the end of a race. The runner should start to slow down only after he has passed the base. A common fault of many runners is that they begin to slow down before reaching the base because they feel they are going to be put out. No runner should ever assume he will be out and should always touch the base. He should never end at the base with a jump, lunge or slide. This will cause him to lose time and he risks chance of injury.

The only time you should allow your runner to slide into first base is when the first baseman leaves the base to take a throw. If the runner has enough time, he can slide either to the inside or outside to avoid a tag.

After running through the base and stopping, the runner should turn to his right or into foul territory. By doing this he will be sure that he does not give the impression that he is making an attempt to go to second base.

The runner should listen to the first base coach while he is running. The coach will alert him if there is a wild throw and he wants him to attempt to go to second base.

TURNS

There are two types of turns that we like to teach our players. The first, we will call the veer out. This is the most common turn used by base runners.

Veer Out

As the runner is approaching first base and he knows the ball is in the outfield, he must prepare to make the turn. When the runner is approximately 20 to 25 feet from the base, he is going to get his body under control. To get his body under control, he must slow down slightly, and veer out to the right. The runner should be watching the front inside corner of the base. This is where he wants to touch the base. He should dip the left shoulder slightly toward the infield so that he can get his momentum going directly toward second base. As the runner hits the base, with either foot, he should push off hard in the direction of second base. The base can be a big help in getting the runner back to full speed after he has gotten his body under control to make the turn.

There are two techniques for touching the base on the turn. If the last step before touching the base is with the left foot (Photo 8-2), the runner touches the base on the inside corner with the right foot and continues on toward second base.

Photo 8-2   **Photo 8-3**

If the last step before touching the base is with the right foot (Photo 8-3), then the runner touches the base with the left foot. In order to get himself going toward second base in a straight line, the runner must throw the right hip over and bring the right arm across his body. This will get his momentum going directly to second base.

Extra Base Hit Turn

The second turn that we teach is used when the runner knows he has hit a ball that has a possibility of being an extra base hit. As the runner leaves the batter's box, he begins to swerve to the right immediately. He should get himself into a position on the grass in foul territory as soon as he leaves the box. By doing this his angle on the turn will be cut down and he will not have to get his body under control as he reaches first base. He should touch the base in the same manner as was discussed in the veer-out turn.

You should instill the aggressive attitude in your players so that they are never satisfied with a single. *Every ball is a double until the defense dictates otherwise!* Once the defense returns the ball to the infield, then and only then, does the runner retreat to first base.

Aggressive Turn Around First Base

You want your runner to make an aggressive turn around first base in order to give the impression that he is making an attempt to go to second base. On a base hit to left field, the runner should be extremely aggressive in rounding first base. The runner should make the turn and go approximately 30 to 35 feet toward second base. If the left fielder bobbles the ball, then the runner can continue on to second base. If the left fielder catches the ball cleanly and returns it to the infield, the runner plants hard on his right foot and retreats to first base. He should retreat to first base watching the ball at all times. If the ball is mishandled by the cutoff man, then the runner can go directly to second base because there is no cutoff man between left field and first base. On a ball hit to center field, the runner should still make an aggressive turn, but he must be more careful because the center fielder could possibly throw behind him. On a ball hit to right field the runner must be careful because now the right fielder can throw behind him. His turn should still be aggressive, but it should be shortened. The runner's technique in stopping after making the turn is to plant on the left foot. He does this so that he can keep sight of the right fielder and the ball as he is returning to first base.

RUNNER ON FIRST BASE

Now that the runner has returned safely to first base, he should listen to the coach for instructions and information. The coach should tell the runner the score, number of outs, game situation and which player has the ball. The runner should never leave the base unless he knows where the ball is.

The runner should look for the signal while he is on the base. This will avoid him getting picked off.

Once the runner has received the signal and gotten all the information from the first base coach, he is now ready to take his lead.

THE CROSSOVER STEP

Before getting into the mechanics of types of leads, it is very important that we discuss the crossover step. This is probably the most important step in baseball. It is used not only in baserunning, but also in infield and outfield play.

Once the runner has reached his maximum lead, he is looking at the pitcher, and is in his baserunning stance. His feet are shoulder width apart; he is on the balls of his feet and his body weight is evenly distributed.

Photo 8-4

To execute the crossover step, the runner pivots on the right foot (he does not lift the foot) and crosses over with the left foot directly toward second base. The runner should not straighten up and then pivot; this will cause him to lose time.

At St. John's we have eliminated the pivot altogether in the crossover step. By eliminating the pivot we save time and also eliminate the possibility of the runner standing up before taking the crossover step. To eliminate the pivot we have the runner point the right foot at a 45 degree angle toward second base. We call this opening the front toe (Photo 8-4). This will feel a bit awkward at first, but after practicing it for a while, it will become comfortable. As the runner is going to break for second base, he does not need to pivot; he can just lean into the crossover step. As he begins to lean, he pushes off on the right foot, throws the left arm across the body toward second base, and gets himself into full stride as quickly as possible.

LEADS

The runner should take his lead by shuffling off the base. By shuffling, we mean he should bring one foot to the other. He should *not* cross his legs. He should have his knees bent, hands off the knees, weight on the balls of the feet and be looking at the pitcher. He should take his lead off the back edge of the base. He does this because when he has to come back to the base, he should come back to the back edge of the base. This is the point farthest from the pitcher and also the point farthest from the first baseman's tag.

The normal lead for most runners is three or four shuffle steps off the base. This is usually in the area of the cut of the infield grass. The size of the lead will be determined by the quickness and agility of the individual runner.

There are three types of leads from first base that we teach. They are the two-way, the one-way, and the walking lead.

The Two-Way Lead

This is the lead used by most runners. By using this lead, the runner has his body weight balanced so that he can go either way. If the pitcher throws to first base, the runner should pivot on the left foot, cross over with the right foot and dive back to the outside corner of the base. If the pitcher throws to the plate and the runner is not stealing, he should cross over and take two or three steps toward second base. This is his secondary lead. He should land on his right foot just as the ball is passing the batter. If the batter hits the ball, then the runner continues on toward second base. This secondary lead also gives the runner a good jump on a passed ball, wild pitch or delayed steal.

If the hitter takes the pitch or swings and misses, then the runner plants hard on the right foot, pivots on the left foot and uses the crossover step back toward first base.

One-Way Lead

This lead is used early in the game when you want the pitcher to throw over to first base. By having the pitcher throw to first base, the runners get a chance to see the pitcher's pickoff move and discover any flaws in the move.

The runner should take his normal lead plus one more step. His weight should be leaning toward first base. As soon as the pitcher makes any move, whether it be toward first base or home plate, the first step by the runner is toward first base. If the pitcher continues to give the runner the big lead, without throwing over to first base, then we are going to start running on him. You can then assume that he doesn't like to throw to first base or that he doesn't have a good pickoff move.

The Walking Lead

This is the type of lead that all good base runners strive to get. A good pitcher is taught never to give a runner a walking lead. He *must* make the runner stop. If a pitcher gets automatic and gives only one look to first base, then the runner can time the look and be moving as soon as the pitcher throws to home plate. The runner should shuffle off the base slowly, keeping the body weight under control, and when the pitcher throws to home plate he uses the crossover step with a hard pushoff on the right foot to get himself into full stride as quickly as possible.

THE HIT AND RUN

The runner's objective on the hit-and-run play is to get a good lead, but he should never get picked off in this situation. The hitter's objective is to make contact with the pitch and, if possible, hit behind the runner. The runner's technique should be as follows:

1. As the pitcher throws the ball toward the plate, the runner breaks for second base.

2. On the runner's third step, he should glance over his left shoulder toward home plate. At approximately this time, the ball should be reaching home plate and the runner can see if the hitter has made contact with the ball. If he sees that the ball is hit on the ground, he continues on toward second base. If he sees that the ball is hit in the air, he puts on the brakes and returns to first base. If he does not see what the hitter does, he should look immediately to the third base coach for some instructions.

RUNNER ON SECOND BASE

When the runner has reached second base, we still want him to be aggressive, but he must be a bit more cautious because now he is in scoring position.

The runner is going to take his *primary lead* as the pitcher comes to the set position. By the *primary lead* (Photo 8-5) we mean that, if the pitcher is in the set position and the second baseman is straddling the base, the runner can get back to the base easily if the pitcher turns

Photo 8-5

to throw to second base. In most cases the second baseman will not be straddling the bag, so the runner can usually get one or two more steps on his primary lead.

As the pitcher is ready to deliver the ball to the plate, the runner should pivot on the right foot and start to walk toward third base. This is called the *secondary lead*. As the ball is reaching the plate, the runner should land on his right foot. If the hitter takes the pitch or swings and misses, the runner plants hard on the right foot and returns to second base. If the hitter makes contact with the ball, then the runner continues on toward third base.

The general rule for a runner to advance to third base is that only if the ball is hit behind him, should he advance to third base. By the ball being hit behind the runner we mean, that the ball is hit behind the runner's left shoulder as he is reaching the maximum point of his secondary lead. The only exception to this rule is if there is a left-handed pull hitter at the plate and the shortstop is shaded directly behind second base. Anything hit very hard directly at the shortstop could result in a play being made at third base.

There are times when the runner can advance to third base on a ball hit in front of him:

1. On a topped roller or swinging bunt that the third baseman must field, the runner should advance to third base.

2. On a slow ground ball to the third baseman's left that he must charge and field on the infield grass, the runner should advance to third base.

3. On a slow hit ball to the shortstop, where the shortstop has to charge the ball and field it in the baseline. The key to this play is that the runner must be able to get past the shortstop before he fields the ball. If he does this, then the shortstop will have to change direction and throw either around or over the runner going to third base.

4. On a ball hit into the hole at shortstop or directly over third base where the shortstop and third baseman have to backhand the ball and come up throwing very quickly. In this situation the shortstop and third baseman do not have time to check the runner at second base. As the shortstop or third baseman release the ball toward first base, then the runner should advance to third base. The key to this play is that the runner on second base "sees the white." This means he sees the ball leave the fielder's hand. We don't want him fooled by a fake throw.

RUNNER ON THIRD BASE

The runner should take a short lead in foul territory. The reason for this is so that if he is hit by a batted ball, he will not be called out. If he is hit in fair territory, he is out.

The runner should note the position of all infielders and out-fielders. He should be aware of the game situations, number of outs, etc.

As the pitcher starts his windup, the runner should begin taking a *walking lead* toward home plate. He should walk aggressively in a slight crouch facing home plate. As the ball reaches the plate, the runner should be landing on his right foot. If the hitter takes the pitch or swings and misses, the runner should plant hard on the right foot and return directly to third base in fair territory. We want the runner inside the foul line so that if the catcher wants to throw to third base, then he has to throw around or over the runner. The runner should watch the third baseman's eyes when returning to third base. This will also let him know if the ball is being thrown to the third base-man.

If the ball is hit, then the runner continues on toward home plate, looking to the on-deck hitter for instructions to stand up or slide.

TAGGING UP

A runner should tag up on all fly balls or line drives with less than two outs. On all fly balls or line drives to left field, center field or right field, the runner should place his left foot on the base and watch the fielder make the catch. The runner can leave the base as soon as the ball hits any part of the fielder.

On fly balls hit in foul territory down the left field line, the runner should place his right foot on the base and watch the fielder make the catch.

LEGAL THIEVERY:
STEALING A BASE

Keep Eyes Open for Extra Bases!

Remind your players: *Every single is a double until the defense proves it is a single.* This also holds true for doubles and triples. Your runners should always be alert and aggressive—ready to take the extra base. Every runner on base should use his eyes and his brain. He should *always* know the score, number of outs, field conditions, what inning it is, his own foot speed, and the ball and strike count.

The base runner should remember that 90 percent of base coaching is done before the ball has been pitched. He should not just wait for the base coach, he should *think!* The base runner should react to anticipated events, be inquisitive, keep alert. The base runner's job is not finished until he has scored!

Taking Advantage of Errors

The base runner should always have a touch of larceny in his heart—alert enough to steal an extra base whenever the opposition fumbles or misplays the ball. Whenever it is apparent that the ball has been thrown over the relay man's head or the cutoff man's head, the runner should advance an extra base. And there is no such thing as an automatic or routine out. At that moment the other team may make the error that will lose them the ball game. Teach your players to run as fast and as aggressively as they can in every situation.

Stealing Second Base

In order to steal a base, a runner does not need great speed. It helps, but it is not the most important ingredient. A base runner must be aggressive, not afraid to take a chance. He must have good powers of concentration and the ability to analyze both the pitcher and the catcher.

Ninety percent of stolen bases are achieved because the pitcher has some flaw in his delivery that gives the runner a good break off first base.

The base runner should take his lead off the back corner of the base in a direct line with second base. His lead will be determined by his own quickness and agility. A rule of thumb for most runners is to take a lead that will give them one step and a dive back to the base. This lead may vary depending on the type of pitcher on the mound, such as a right or left-handed pitcher, good pickoff move, poor pickoff move, etc.

The runner should use the crossover step with the open toe when attempting to steal a base.

Tip-offs by the right-handed pitcher

Raising heel of left leg. When the pitcher raises the heel of the left leg, he usually delivers the ball to home plate.

Turning left shoulder. When the pitcher's left shoulder moves in the direction of third base, he must then deliver the ball to home plate.

Breaking hands in middle of stretch position. Many pitchers will throw to first base by breaking the hands on the way down to the belt. Once they reach the belt they deliver the ball to home plate.

One look. Many times pitchers become automatic and only look once at the runner. When this happens the runner can get a tremendous jump by breaking as soon as the pitcher turns his head.

There are many other tip-offs by individual pitchers, and each runner should study the pitcher from the dugout and try to pick out his one fault to give him the best possibility of stealing the base.

Tip-offs by the left-handed pitcher

Looking at you. If the left-handed pitcher is looking at the runner, he has a tendency to deliver the ball to home plate.

Looking at plate. If the left-handed pitcher is looking at home plate, he has a tendency to throw to first base.

Break plane of rubber. If the left-handed pitcher breaks the plane of the pitching rubber with his right foot, then he must deliver the ball to home plate.

Good move to first. If a left-handed pitcher has a very good move to first base, then the runner can guess and hope that the pitcher is going to deliver the ball to home plate. When most left-handed pitchers raise their right leg, they have already made up their mind if they are throwing to home or first base. If the runner guesses right, he gets a great jump; if he guesses wrong, he should go as hard as he can all the way into second base. The runner should try to beat the throw from the first baseman.

Toe pointing up. If the left-handed pitcher has the toe of his right foot pointing up, he usually throws to home plate.

Toe pointing down. If the left-handed pitcher has the toe of his right foot pointing down, he usually throws to first base.

Again, there are many tip-offs, but you must pick out the one that will benefit you most.

Stealing Third Base

Third base is the easiest base to steal. Many teams do not hold runners close to second base; therefore, the runner can get a longer lead off the base. Many pitchers tend to get more automatic with a runner on second base.

The base runner should get a good primary lead and listen to the third base coach for directions and help. A good base runner will get a walking lead off second base. A runner should not attempt to steal third base unless he gets a walking lead. If the runner is leaning toward second base or is standing still, he should not attempt the steal.

It is not advisable to steal third base with a left-handed hitter at bat or with two outs.

SLIDING

Sliding is a controlled way of falling and stopping. In order to execute any type of slide, the body must be relaxed. The hands and arms should be off the ground and the force of the slide should be directed aggressively toward the base.

If you are thinking of sliding into a base, *do it*. Never hesitate or change your mind in the middle of a slide—this can cause serious injury.

Coaches should be very emphatic in their directions and commands to slide. If there is any chance of a play—*slide!*

Some of the reasons for sliding are to:

1. avoid a putout
2. stop momentum
3. avoid overrunning a base
4. avoid injury

Types of Slides

Bent leg or stand up slide

If a player wants to get up quickly after sliding, he should use the bent-leg slide. This will enable the runner to advance to the next base on an error or an overthrow. The execution of the bent-leg slide is as follows:

1. The runner should approach the base and at approximately 10′ to 12′ from the base he should begin his slide.

2. Both feet should leave the ground at about the same time and the right leg should be extended straight out toward the base. The left leg should bend under the right leg with the instep of the left foot turned to the side so as not to catch the spikes in the dirt.

3. The runner should have his hands raised and back at a 45-degree angle off the ground (sitting position).

4. The runner should hit the base with the heel of the right foot and push up with the left leg into a standing position. This will allow him to stop on the base or advance in case of an overthrow.

Illustration 8-1

Hook slide (Illustration 8-1)

The hook slide is used to avoid a tag and should be mastered to both sides of the base. It is executed as follows:

1. At approximately 10 to 12 feet from the base, the runner should start his slide. The lead leg on the takeoff will be the leg that hooks the base.
2. The body falls into a supine position (the runner is lying flat on his back and hands in the air).
3. The base is contacted by the lead foot (instep of inside foot).
4. The body and the other leg should continue past the base with the toe of the inside foot maintaining contact with the base.

The runner should watch the positioning and eyes of the fielder to determine in which direction he should slide to evade the tag. The runner should also listen to the directions of the coach to help him determine the direction of the slide.

Straight-in slide (Illustration 8-2)

This slide is very much like the Bent-Leg Slide and should be used when the runner wants to get to the base as quickly as possible. When the play is going to be close, the runner should go straight in and not try the hook slide, which makes the runner slide a longer distance to the base.

Illustration 8-2

The head first slide or dive

Many players have taken to the Head First Slide because it is quicker, but it is also more dangerous. The runner can take off from approximately 15 feet from the base. He should be running at full speed and should glide into the Head First Slide. The runner should not bellywhop or jump into the dive. The runner's hands and arms should be extended with the hands and arms relaxed. The brunt of the slide should be taken by the runner's chest and abdomen. The thighs and feet should be slightly off the ground. The hands should grab the base with the wrist at a 45-degree angle so as not to jam the fingers straight into the base.

Teaching Sliding

All players should be taught to slide, just for the sake of avoiding injury. Each player should be able to master at least one slide completely, but should try to master all the slides. The players must first learn to *slide—not jump*. Take sliding and break it down into stages. Have the players remove their spikes and wear sweat pants and sliding pads.

Stage 1: sit down through the slide

Have the players sit on the ground and sit in the position of each slide in sequence.

Stage 2: fall into slide

After sitting through the slide, have the players stand up and fall into the position of the slide.

Stage 3: slow motion

Place a movable base on a soft, level, grassy area in the outfield. You can take a hose and wet the area down to allow the players to slide farther and easier.

Stage 4: full speed

As players become more adept at sliding, follow the same procedure as the Slow Motion. At this point you can have contests with the players as to who can slide the longest distance, best technique, etc.

TIPS FOR SLIDERS

1. When leading off a base, pick up dirt in both hands. This will serve as a reminder to keep hands and arms off the ground and will help avoid wrist jamming and slide burns of the hands and arms; or wear batting gloves on both hands.

2. When sliding, always keep your spikes turned to the side or up to avoid catching them in the ground. This will prevent foot, ankle, and leg injuries.

3. Take off point should be between 10 to 15 feet from the base according to the type of slide required.

4. Watch the eyes and positioning of the fielder to determine which direction you should slide.

5. Listen to the coach and watch his actions for instructions on which direction to slide.

6. Be ready to stand up and advance further on an overthrow, fumble, or continuing play.

7. Beware of the decoy and quick tag.

8. Take out slides are meant to harass or throw an opponent off balance— *never to injure!*

9. When in doubt, *slide!*

10. *Never* change your mind in the middle of a slide. This can result in injury.

11. Do not jump into a slide—glide into the slide!

ALL-PURPOSE BASERUNNING DRILL

This drill is used to practice baserunning techniques and also to improve the general conditioning of players. The drill begins with the whole team, pitchers included, lined up behind home plate facing first base.

Home to first base: Each player steps into the batter's box, right-handed hitters in the right-hand box and left-handed hitters in the left-hand box. The first player steps into the batter's box and takes a simulated swing. He gets out of the batter's box by stepping toward first base with the back foot. He then uses good running form as he runs along the foul line toward first base. As he approaches first base, he touches the top front portion of the base with either foot. The runner should not break stride as he runs through the base. He should run to a point 15 to 20 feet past the base and turn to his right into foul territory. He then walks back toward home plate. Each player on the team follows the same routine.

Round first base and comeback, watching the ball: The first player on the line steps into the batter's box, swings and runs to first base. As he approaches first base, approximately 25 feet from the base, he begins his veer-out turn. He should touch the base with either foot without breaking stride. He should make an aggressive turn around first base and go approximately 30 feet toward second base. He should stop by planting on the right foot and return to first base while keeping his eyes on the ball at all times.

Round first base, hesitate and go to second base: The first player steps into the batter's box, swings and runs to first base. As he approaches the base, he uses the veer-out turn, touches the base, makes the aggressive turn and plants on the right foot to stop. As he starts back toward first base, he is watching the ball. He takes two or three steps toward first base, plants hard on the left foot and heads toward second base. This part of the drill simulates the outfielder bobbling the ball or overthrowing the cutoff man.

Lead-off first base: All players line up by first base coaching box. The first player takes his lead. He uses the crossover step and simulates stealing second base. When he is about 20 feet from second base, the runner glances over his left shoulder and looks to the third base coach for a signal to continue on to third or hold at second. This also gives the third base coach a chance to practice giving signs to the runners.

Lead-off second base and score on a base hit: The players line up behind second base and the first player takes his primary lead off second base. He then takes his secondary lead and breaks toward third base. As he approaches third base, he should listen to the third base coach for a verbal sign and watch him for a visual sign as to whether he should continue to home plate or stop at third base.

Tag up at third base: All players line up behind third base. Each player then takes his walking lead in foul territory, lands on his right foot, and simulates a fly ball being hit to the outfield. He plants on the right foot and returns to third base to tag up. Using the proper tag-up technique, the runner tags up and runs hard toward home plate to score the run.

Run to second base on a double: All players line up at home plate again and the first player takes his simulated swing. He uses the proper technique of getting out of the batter's box, makes the proper turn at first base, and runs hard all the way to second base.

Run to third base on a triple: Follow the same procedure as running to second base, only the runner continues to third base.

Run from home to home: Use same procedure as running to second base and third base. This time the runner is running out an inside the park home run.

Home run trot: This part of the drill can be a lot of fun. After doing the baserunning drills, let the players practice their home run trot after hitting a ball out of the park. It's interesting to check the different styles of each player and the comments by the other players and members of the coaching staff.

BASERUNNING TIPS

1. Run at full speed until the defense makes you stop.
2. Touch all the bases!
3. Stay on the base until the pitcher is on the rubber.
4. "Go for two" on every base hit that goes between the third baseman and the third baseline or the first baseman and the first baseline.
5. Hustle back to the base as soon as you know that the ball has been positively caught by the catcher.
6. Watch the man ahead of you. It's embarrassing to have two base runners occupying the same base.
7. If you are ever in doubt, *slide*. Slide often and slide aggressively. Go get 'em.

Going to second

8. On extra base hits, the runner should follow a modified circle route. He should touch the corner of the base that is

nearest to the pitcher's mound, with the foot that gets there first.

9. With runners on first and third bases and one out, the runner going from first base to second base on a ground ball to the second baseman should *never* allow the second baseman to tag him out.

10. With two outs, runners on first and second base, or with the bases loaded, the runner on first base should get a good jump so that he can beat the force play at second base. Take the easy play away from them.

The runner on second

11. The runner on second base *must* score in the following situations:

   a. Two outs and a base hit that leaves the infield

   b. A ground ball base hit to the left of the runner that leaves the infield

   c. Any ground ball base hit that leaves the infield regardless of the number of outs, with first base occupied

12. With less than two out and no one on first base, the runner on second base should make sure all ground balls to his right go through the infield before he advances to third base. His position as a base runner will be the line of demarcation that decides whether or not he should run on ground balls. The runner should advance to third base on all ground balls hit to his left that get by the pitcher. It is also important for him to advance to third base on a slow hit or on a short, high hopping ground ball that causes the third baseman to advance ten feet or more onto the infield grass.

Going from third to home

13. The runner on third base with less than two outs must tag up on *all* fly balls to the outfield that have even a remote possibility of being caught.

14. Unless instructed differently by the coach, a runner on third base with one out, regardless of the position of the infielders, should go for home on every ground ball!

15. On a line drive, the runner must *never* get doubled up! For

the runner on third base, with no outs, to be doubled up on a line drive must be considered the *unpardonable sin*.

When base runners need to be careful

16. When your team is behind by two or more runs, your players should never try to take the extra base or put the ball club in jeopardy by doing something foolish. Remind them that "catch-up" baseball is the hardest kind to play. This is no time to do anything stupid to intensify the problem that already exists.

AGGRESSIVE BASE COACHING

Coaching the bases is a skill that must be learned and practiced, as any other skill in baseball. An above-average to superior base coach can mean the difference between winning and losing a game. Having good base coaches gives a team the equal of two extra players on the field.

Not everyone is suited to base coaching. It requires the following qualities:

- the giving of oneself to the team—too often the base coaching job goes unnoticed.
- an above-average knowledge of the game.
- the ability to make quick, accurate decisions, based on sound judgment.
- the ability to lead.

Be ready to develop these qualities by working with those individuals who really want to give of themselves, because not every team has an assistant or two. Give your base coaches every chance to learn. Participating in situation team drills will provide the learning base coaches with the opportunities to practice their movements. They will also get the opportunity to familiarize themselves with the capabilities of various players on the team.

Let's look at factors that must be learned and understood by the base coaches and the players, and the movements that a base coach must learn to do his job effectively.

THE FIRST BASE COACH

Let's begin at the first base coaching box. Infield hits and extra bases may depend primarily on the runner's hustle and speed, but an active first base coach can have an important bearing on the runner's effort. You are looking for that little "extra" and you want the first base coach to keep the runners aware and alert at all times. The runners appreciate a base coach who tells them what to do because they realize they both are seeking the same objective—a hit.

The following are some directions that a first base coach may shout to motivate and assist base runners:

"Run hard!" (or similar shouts such as: "Dig it," or "Straight through the base.") The runner should respond by running all out and through the base, touching the base at its nearest edge. These commands signal that all the effort by the runner should be made to beat the throw to the base. A turn to the right and a return to first are all that is required after the runner has passed the bag.

"Turn and hold." This is used when the coach wants the runner to round first base. He points with his right hand to second base and shouts, "turn and hold." The coach also tells the runner where the ball is being fielded. The runner, upon leaving the batter's box, begins his turn about halfway down the base path. He runs a few feet to the right of the base line in foul territory and turns into the base. The runner should be taught never to break stride and stop his movement about 12 to 14 feet from the base or sooner as he picks up the player fielding the ball. On occasion, further advancement is possible because of a misplay by the defense.

"Turn and look." This is another shout to bring about a reaction on the part of the runner. The first base coach does the same as the "Turn and hold" drill except he now shouts "turn and look" and points only to the field where the ball has been hit. The "cue" here is *look*. The runner, when he hears this, knows he can go a little further than the previous play, approximately 20 to 25 feet beyond first base, and here he evaluates the situation. The coach can continue to assist the base runner verbally, but the ability of the base runner to react to the defense is important. Additional advancement is more common here because the aggressive behavior of the runner often causes the defense to make mistakes.

"Take two and look!" Whenever there is a sure extra base hit, the coach will move his left arm vigorously and point to second base with

the right arm. The verbal cue of *"take two and look"* means just that. The runner never breaks stride and continues to second base; he should pick up the third base coach for a signal only if he cannot see the play in front of him. Remember, the base runner begins his turn much sooner than the previous drill, because he knows he is going on to second base.

Additional first base responsibilities

Let's look at some additional responsibilities of the first base coach when he has a runner on first or second base. With the runner at first base, the first base coach will:

- Keep runner aware of the situation.
- Remind runner of the pitcher's best pickoff move.
- Tell the runner where the ball is at all times.
- Remind the runner of the strengths and weaknesses of the outfield.
- Keep the runner informed of what he should do if there is a hit. When there is a runner on second base, all of the above are important as well as keeping the runner aware of the location of the keystone players (shortstop and second baseman).

THE THIRD BASE COACH

The challenge at third is even greater than at first base. Mistakes can cause a game to be lost, but if you follow a few simple rules you may be able to keep the mistakes to a minimum.

The third base coach should start off in the coach's box. He is supposed to remain in the box, but we all know he will roam as far as the umpires allow. Usually on hits the umpires will disregard the third base coach's movement, but not so when he tries to roam to pick off the catcher's signals. The rule of thumb to follow is to go as far as the officials permit.

A third base coach should use simple and easy to see signals and give the runners sufficient time to react.

The following are some examples and drills that should be practiced.

Stand Up

The runner who is approaching second or third base does not have the play in front of him. The third base coach raises both hands with palms facing the runner. This signal is given to the base runner early enough to prevent him from overrunning the base.

As at first base, the runner coming into second must be aware of what signals to look for from the third base coach. These signals will assist the runner in reaching third base and possibly home safely:

Stop at second! If the third base coach wants the runner to stop at second base, not even to round the base, he should raise the left hand with the palm facing the runner. The right hand should be pointing directly at second base.

Stay and return! The coach, by moving his left arm in a circular motion, informs the runner to round second base and be prepared to advance to third or return to second. The decision is made by the third base coach as the runner rounds the base. Two hands up and palms facing the runner signals him to stay and return; left arm circling with hand pointing to third base means *to keep coming.*

Come to third without stopping. If the third base coach wants the runner to come to third base without any hesitation, his right arm circles vigorously as the runner approaches second base. The coach should also position himself closer to third base in case he must instruct the runner with another signal (such as stand up or slide).

Watching keystone. With a runner on second base, we believe the third base coach should focus his attention on the keystone combination. The runner should assume a lead long enough to allow him to beat the pitcher's throw if the pitcher attempts to pick him off. This allows each runner the opportunity to lead according to his ability; it also allows the coach the easy task of watching the keystone combination and not shouting continuously. We believe this is quite easy because it allows the runner to react to the pitcher. If the pitcher begins to throw to home plate, the runner can move further off the bag. If the pitcher attempts to pick him off, the runner should return to second base.

"It must go through" is the basic cue to the runner on second base concerning a ground ball to the left side. If this rule is followed, a runner should never be thrown out at third base on a ground ball to the left side with less than two outs. The third base coach will also remind the runner to tag up on fly balls.

Reacting to a Tag Up

When the ball is hit, coach shouts "tag up!" The runner returns to third base, locates the ball and reacts to the catch. We do not believe the coach should offer any other assistance other than telling the runner to hold if the fly ball is not deep enough for a successful tag up. Remember, it is quicker and safer for the runner to react to a catch than for a coach to yell "go." Everyone reacts to it and sometimes the "go" registers an early take off to the umpire. It is a rare ball that a runner cannot locate for a tag up. Only when this occurs is further assistance necessary from a third base coach.

Other Communicating Signals

The slide signal is palms down; if the runner can stand up, the hand pointed to base is acceptable and easy to see. On a hit to the outfield with a runner on second base, the third base coach moves up the line toward home plate. This gives him more time to make a decision. As the runner drives through the base at top speed the coach either waves him on or sends him back to the base with his hands up and yelling "back."

Coaching tips with a runner on third base and less than two outs

- The runner should return to third base immediately on all infield line drives. If the ball is not caught, the runner will score.
- When the ball is pitched, the runner should be in foul territory.
- When the catcher receives the ball, runner should step back into the playing field (fair ground).
- Return to tag up position on all fly balls. If the ball falls in, the runner will score. However, if the runner returns after the catch, he will be too late in tagging up.
- Remember, the coach and players will react from third base as the head coach desires. Some teams are more aggressive than others. This is where individual team characteristics come into play.

The *on-deck coach* is just that; he is the next batter or previous runner. Communication is important. The same signals as previously mentioned are used. The on-deck coach must make sure he does not interfere with the catcher or umpire. The effort and time put into these few examples of proper base coaching will be a worthwhile investment for game situations. The team with the most runs wins the game, and if excellent base coaching is the source of more runs, let's make sure your team has them.

HITTING:
Using the Contact Spot

9

In order to be successful, each batter must go up to home plate with an aggressive attitude, and then concentrate on making contact with the ball. He must have learned two important things about himself—first, what his role is as a hitter, and second, what pitch in what part of the strike zone he can handle best.

If your player is one of those rare individuals who is strong enough and accurate enough to hit home runs often, his role is that of the heavy hitter. Unless he is capable of consistently hitting the ball out of the park, however, his aim should be to hit line drives and not fly balls. If your player is small and not strong in stature, he should work on his ability to spray the ball to all fields, to hit to move runners up, to bunt well and to get himself on base any way he can.

Knowing what pitch he can handle best is important, so when your player is at bat he can wait for and look for that pitch. Smart hitters get their hits from pitchers' mistakes; when a pitcher makes a mistake, all the hitter has to do is take advantage of it. If he can do this three out of ten times, he will be considered a good hitter. It is also important for him to discipline himself to swing only at pitches in the strike zone. If the batter swings at bad pitches, he gives the pitcher every advantage, because he is enlarging the strike zone and the pitcher is getting him to swing at his pitch more often.

There are many different stances and styles of hitting, but all good hitters wind up the same way when they make contact with the ball. The important thing in hitting is to be comfortable and on balance throughout the swing. Good head position, along with a swing that allows the hitter to drive the ball, will result in the formula for successful hitting.

WHAT IS THE CONTACT SPOT?

The contact spot is the spot where the bat and the ball meet. Every good hitter winds up the same way: his arms are extended, the back hip is open, the barrel of the bat is about 90 degrees even with his hands, and with his wrists not yet broken before contact. The weight is transferred into a braced front leg, and the back toe and knee are pointed at the pitcher with the heel off the ground, and the head is down looking at the contact spot (Illustration 9-1).

Illustration 9-1

In order to be a good hitter the batter must get into this contact spot consistently as the ball arrives there. Some hitters can take a long swing and still be consistently in the contact spot while others must shorten their swing and become more compact in order to be successful. Each hitter must learn for himself his quickness and reaction time to get into the contact spot. Once he establishes this, he has the type of swing needed to be a good hitter.

THE MECHANICS OF HITTING

The mechanics of hitting are broken down into the following phases:

Selecting a bat

Grip

Stance

Position of the hands

Where to stand in the batter's box

Stride

Swing

Rotation of the hips

Follow-through

Let's look at each of these elements in detail.

Selecting a Bat

Each player must discover for himself what type of bat is best for him. A hitter should find a bat that feels good in his hands. He should pick it up and see whether it is balanced and that the handle is the right size for his hands. Remember, a bat is nothing more than extension of the hitter's arms; the hitter should be able to swing it and not let it swing him. If a bat is too heavy, the bat head will drag behind the hands or cause the top hand to fall below the bottom hand, resulting in an uppercut swing.

Grip

The grip should be comfortable and firm, not tense and tight. The bat is gripped in the fingers rather than in the palms of the hands. A relaxed grip is essential for quickness and power. A tight grip tends to tighten up the forearm and wrist muscles, thus reducing flexibility.

When the hitter swings the bat the grip tightens automatically providing maximum power at the right time.

There are basically three different kinds of grips used in hitting (Illustration 9-2). One is the *regular grip*, where the bottom hand is down at the end of the bat. Another grip is called a *modified grip*, where the bottom hand is about two or three inches up from the bottom; and the third is the *choked grip*, where the bottom hand is about four to six inches from the end. Whatever grip the hitter uses, the same principles apply as far as tightness and holding the bat in the fingers is concerned.

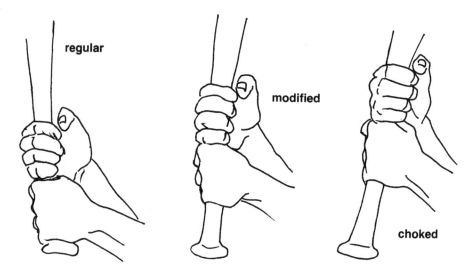

Illustration 9-2

Stance

The best stance is the one that is the most comfortable and keeps the hitter balanced at all times. There are three basic positions from which a hitter can start (Illustration 9-3). First, there is an *open stance*, where the front foot opens the body facing the pitcher. Second, there is a *closed stance*, where the front foot points more towards first base (right-handed hitter). The third stance is a *squared stance*, where both feet are on an even line.

The importance of the stance is not in how the hitter starts, but in how he winds up in the contact spot. In teaching a basic stance you should suggest that the feet be about shoulder width apart. Make sure the player's body weight is distributed equally and on the balls of the

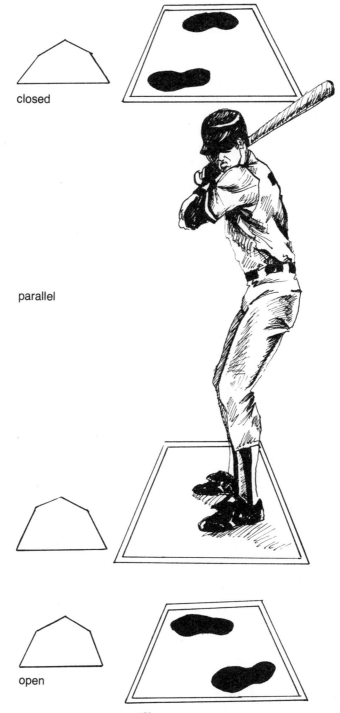

closed

parallel

open

Illustration 9-3

feet. The head should be stationary with both eyes facing the pitcher. Hips and shoulders must be kept level, with the front hip and shoulder pointing at the pitcher. Hands are generally held about chest high and back behind the rear foot. Knees are slightly bent, helping the hitter to relax. A hitter can move quickly and maintain better control of his body if he starts in a relaxed position rather than a tense one. Many hitters like to have some movement in their body as they are in their stance enabling them to get some rhythm just before the swing. This is called *never starting from still*. It generally keeps the body more relaxed. Some hitters do this by a slight sway with the knees or hands by moving back and forth until they're ready to swing. As mentioned before, the importance of the stance is to start in a comfortable position on balance and wind up in the contact spot consistently.

Position of the Hands

Where the hitter's hands start in the stance is not as important as where they wind up in the completion of the stride. It is very important that the hands remain back as the stride leg lands. In most cases, the hands generally start about chest high and a little back of the rear leg. As the hitter gets ready to swing, the wrists are cocked, the hands are back and ready to explode at the ball.

Where to Stand in the Batter's Box

A hitter will either stand in the back of the box, up in front of the box or in the middle. The type of pitcher will determine your position (Illustration 9-4). For example, with a pitcher who throws hard and mostly fast balls, the hitter usually stays deep back in the box. This gives the hitter a split second longer to see the ball and his chance of being constantly jammed on the inside pitch is lessened.

For a pitcher who throws mostly curve balls, the hitter can move up toward the front of the box, so he can reach the ball before its full break. Remember: The closer the hitter is to home plate, and up in the batter's box, the quicker he must be in getting his bat to the ball on the inside pitch.

Stride

The stride is a timing mechanism that reminds the hitter to keep his body weight back. As the stride leg lands, the hands and body weight

Illustration 9-4

must remain back until the swing brings everything forward. A common fault among many hitters is to stride too far, which causes them to lunge at the ball. If the hitter's body gets out in front or ahead of the swing, the hands will have a difficult time in catching up. This will result in a bat drag, where the barrel of the bat is behind the hands, losing all driving power during contact. The hitter who usually takes a short stride has better control of his forward motion, is properly balanced, and maintains better eye contact with the ball. The longer the stride, the more chance he has of dropping his eye level. With a short stride he can wait longer on the ball and adjust quicker to different types of pitches. Again, the purpose of the stride is to keep the weight on the rear foot until the swing is started.

Swing (Illustration 9-5)

Illustration 9-5

There are basically two different opinions on what type of swing to use. Some hitting instructors say swing "slightly up" and some believe in a slight downward swing. *Remember*, the bat must be in the contact spot as the ball gets there. The shorter and more compact the swing, the quicker the hitter can get into the contact spot. This shortens the distance the bat has to travel.

The swing that is slightly upward is usually longer and requires the bat to travel a greater distance. Home run and power hitters usually swing in this fashion. We believe a good swing should be as nearly level as possible.

Before the swing starts, the hands are back, wrists are cocked and ready to throw the bat into the ball. As the swing starts, the body weight is shifted from the ball of the back foot onto the ball of the front foot. The head of the bat is whipped or snapped into the contact spot with the arms extended. The rear foot turns with the knee and toes pointing toward the pitcher. This shifts the weight forward and opens his hips to let the arms come through. This gives the batter full power of the arms and body. The weight is then transferred into a braced front leg with the arms extended and wrists not turned over. The head remains down looking at the contact spot. During the swing, the front arm guides the bat and the top hand does the snapping. The hitter hits the ball before his wrists break. The force of the head of the bat is what turns the wrists over.

Rotation of the Hips

Along with the wrists and arms, batting power comes from rotating the hips. Rotating the hips (Photo 9-1)—moving them out of the way

Photo 9-1

and letting the momentum and power of the body come forward into the swing—is one of the most important movements in hitting. For good hip rotation, the rear foot must turn as though it were facing the pitcher; as it turns, it forces the hips to open. This opening of the hips brings the hands and body through to transfer the weight forward.

Follow-Through

After the hips and wrists have whipped through and the player has hit the ball, a complete follow-through (Photo 9-2) is necessary. A complete follow-through provides power to the swing and gives distance to the hits. After contact, the bat continues under its own momentum to the rear of the body.

Photo 9-2

The follow-through is from shoulder to shoulder with both the bat and the player's head. The hitter should now be in perfect balance, with the body facing the direction of the ball just hit. This enables the batter to start toward first base with his rear foot taking the first step.

COMPLETE REVIEW OF THE BATTING METHOD: A CHECKLIST FOR BATTING

Going to the Plate

——— Select a bat that is comfortable for your swing.

——— Grip the bat comfortably and firm, not tense and tight.

———— Grip the bat in the fingers, not back in the palm, and grip it where you can swing it best.

———— Assume a comfortable stance that keeps you on balance at all times.

Batting Position

———— Body weight should be evenly distributed on the balls of the feet.

———— Head should be stationary with both eyes on the pitcher and the ball.

———— Hips and shoulders should be level, with the front hip and shoulder pointing at the pitcher.

———— Knees should be slightly bent, helping you to relax.

———— Butt and hips should not be sticking out too far.

———— Stance should give you good coverage of the plate.

———— Hands are usually held chest high and just a little back of the rear leg.

———— Wrists are cocked and ready to explode out at the ball.

Swing of the Bat

———— As the swing starts, shift your weight from the back foot so it ends up on the front foot after contact.

———— Whip or snap the head of the bat into the contact spot with your arms extended and away from the body.

———— Your stride should enable you to keep your weight back and not let your body go too far forward.

———— The hips must open to let the momentum and power of the body come forward into the swing.

———— For good hip rotation, the rear foot must turn with the toes facing the pitcher.

The Follow-Through

———— After the hips and wrists have whipped through and hit the ball, a complete follow-through is necessary.

———— The follow-through provides power to the swing, giving you a little extra when the ball is hit.

———— You should be in good balance throughout the entire hitting action.

ZONING YOUR PITCH

Once a hitter has acquired the proper mechanics of hitting, his job becomes 90 percent mental. Every hitter should learn what pitch gives him the best chance for a hit and in what part of the strike zone it is. Every time the count is in his favor he should look for this pitch. This is known as *zoning your pitch* (Illustration 9-6). If the count is no

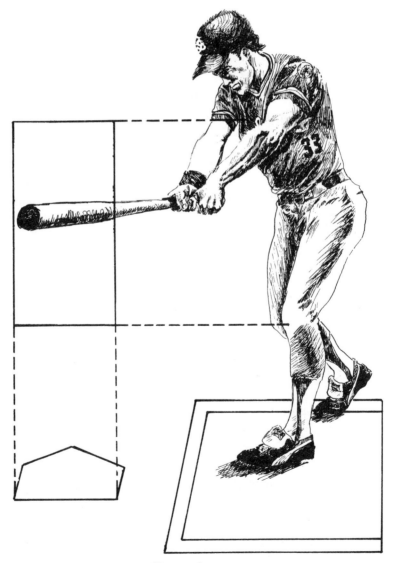

Illustration 9-6

strikes, and the pitcher throws a perfect "pitcher's pitch," if the batter swings he is going against the percentage. He's unlikely to get a good hit. Instead, he should wait for the pitch in his zone.

A pitcher is only human; sooner or later he will make mistakes. A smart hitter capitalizes on this and will take full advantage of any pitching mistake. Most pitchers will not throw three perfect strikes during the player's time at bat. Once that batter sees "his pitch" coming, he should be ready for it. If a pitcher happens to throw his strikes perfectly, the batter can only tip his hat to him, and get him the next time up.

A good rule for the batter to follow when there are no strikes is to look for a pitch in the part of the strike zone he wants. When the count is one strike, the batter enlarges his strike zone a bit, and when the count goes to two strikes, the batter must protect the entire strike zone.

One of the most important things any hitter must learn is to swing only at pitches in the strike zone. Each hitter who swings at pitches outside the strike zone gives that pitcher a much bigger target at which to throw. The pitcher's corners of the plate now become larger, and his pitches become more difficult to handle. Teach your hitters to look for "their pitch," especially when the count is in their favor. They should never swing at a pitch they have trouble handling unless the count forces them. They should swing at tough-to-handle pitches only when the count dictates it.

HITTING DRILLS

Hitting from the Batting "Tee"

A batting tee is usually a home plate with a rubber tubing attached in the middle which runs straight up. It can be adjusted to any height in the strike zone so the hitter can hit both high and low pitches. The tee is placed so that when the hitter swings his bat is in the contact spot. The batter practices his batting mechanics by hitting a ball off the top of the tubing. He concentrates on keeping his head down and eyes on the ball at all times. The object is to hit the ball off the tee with a smooth mechanical swing without making any contact with the rubber tubing. A coach should stand behind the hitter watching, and making any comments that would aid in the improvement of his hitting mechanics. This drill can be used both indoors and outdoors.

Soft Toss Drill (Photo 9-3)

In the Soft Toss Drill a "feeder" player flips the ball to the hitter, who assumes his normal stance as if he were waiting for a pitch to hit. The feeder kneels down, facing the hitter about six feet to his side. The feeder tosses a ball with an underhand flip to the front hip, which is the contact spot. The batter swings and hits the ball into a fence, or wall with padding, using his full hitting mechanics. The coach should stand by and watch, making any suggestions in order to help the hitter. This is a good drill to quicken the hands and open the hips. If a hitter wants to learn how to hit a pitch moving away from him, like a slider or curve ball, the feeder can move to the other side of the hitter where the hitter's back is now to the feeder. The ball is now coming in the direction as if it is moving away from him. Eye contact with the ball is also stressed in this drill.

    If the hitter wants to work on just quickening his hands, he can get down with his rear knee touching the ground and have his front leg extended out and use the same soft toss drill. This drill can be used both indoors and outdoors.

Photo 9-3

THE IMPORTANCE OF BATTING PRACTICE

Batting practice can be used for several purposes. It can be used as a pregame warmup, to allow the hitters to loosen up and be ready for their game. It can be used to teach hitters the correct mechanics of hitting by having a coach watch and suggest anything he feels can aid in helping the hitter. It can also be used for hitters who want to work on different aspects of hitting, such as hitting to the opposite field, fighting their way out of a slump, bunting and practicing hit and run. Whatever the reason, it should be used to aid and improve the hitter.

Batting practice can be done in different ways. It depends on the time you have and number of players involved. Some coaches break their hitters into groups and set a time limit for each group. Other coaches give a specified amount of swings to every hitter.

Generally, a good system to follow is to have your hitter begin by taking two bunts, one down the first base side and the other down the third base side. After he completes the two bunts he then fakes a bunt and slashes, making sure he hits the ball on the ground. Next he then swings at a pitch as if it is hit and run, concentrating on making good hard contact. After completing his bunts, slash, and hit and run, he then takes the specified amount of hits alloted and runs the last hit out as if it were a ground ball to an infielder. He now remains on first base until the next batter bunts. This also gives the runner an opportunity to work on his baserunning by practicing his lead off the base. As the ball is bunted, the base runner moves up to the next base and waits for the next bunt by the batter; on the next bunt he advances to third base.

When on third base, he works on his walking lead in foul territory, watching to see where the next ball will be hit. If the ball is hit on the ground, he breaks toward home plate. If the ball is hit in the air, he goes back to the base and works on tagging up.

Setting up stations for hitting can be beneficial to your hitters. One station can be a batting tee, the next could be soft toss area, and the third could be hitting in a cage. Your hitters can start at station one and move along to all three.

BATTING DRILLS

Playing Pepper

Playing pepper is a good drill for improving hand and eye coordination and bat control. It is also a good drill for fielding ground balls and practicing good fielding mechanics. This drill can be done with two to four players.

A batter and one to three fielders face one another about 25 feet apart, with the fielders next to each other about arms' distance apart. The object is for the batter to hit the ball on the ground to each fielder as they throw the ball to him. The batter hits about 25 to 30 ground balls, concentrating on hitting to each fielder. After he completes his hitting, the batter now becomes a fielder and one of the fielders becomes the new hitter.

Isometric Bat Drill

The batter can use any stationary object that cannot be moved, such as a pole, fence or back stop. The object of this drill is to strengthen the muscles of the arms, wrists and shoulders used in the batting swing.

The batter places his bat against the stationary object while he is in the contact spot of the swing. He now pushes the bat as hard as he can for ten seconds, as if trying to complete the swing.

Swinging a Weighted Bat

This is a good drill used mainly in the off-season to strengthen the muscles used in the swing. A bat that is slightly heavier than the one ordinarily used is swung about 50 times a day. It is a good idea to have each player swing from both sides in order to strengthen the arm, shoulder and wrist muscles. An extremely heavy bat is not recommended, because it can lead to an improper swing. Have the player use a bat light enough to be readily handled, to practice a normal swing.

Stand in the Batter's Box Watching Pitches

This is a good drill so each player will get an idea of the strike zone and the pitches he feels he can handle well. This drill is done when a pitcher warms up in the pen, or is throwing on the side.

The batter gets into his stance in a batter's box while the pitcher is throwing. He just watches the pitches go by without swinging and pictures in his mind the pitches he can handle and the pitches that would give him trouble.

Swinging in Front of a Mirror

This drill helps the hitter see himself and analyze his swing. The batter stands in front of a mirror and swings at imaginary pitches that are high, low, inside and outside in the strike zone. He watches how he swings and sees if he can handle the pitch with the right type of swing. Sometimes a frame "strike zone" can be hung or superimposed on the mirror.

Hip Rotation Drill

This drill is used to encourage the opening of the hips during the batting swing. The hitter assumes his normal stance with his feet. He places his arms behind his back and a bat is placed resting on the forearms. The hitter rotates his hips as if it were an actual swing, using his arms and the bat behind him to help him pop the hips. This helps hitters who have a lazy front hip, or who are slow opening up in attempting to hit the inside pitch.

BUNTING

Bunting is an important part of a team's offense. It is used to move runners along and it is used as a means of getting a base hit. A player who can bunt effectively adds another offensive weapon to his repertoire. It is also important to learn the fake bunt and slash, which is a technique that allows the hitter to fake a bunt and hit away.

A great deal of time and emphasis should be devoted to bunting during practice. Each player must learn to execute a sacrifice bunt successfully, for in the long run, it will pay off by winning many close ball games.

There are two types of bunts used. One is the sacrifice bunt and the other is the bunt for a base hit.

The Sacrifice Bunt

The sacrifice bunt is when a batter must move a runner to the next base. The batter must make sure that he bunts the ball on the ground, and not be concerned about getting a base hit. Sacrifice means giving oneself up to move the runner. There are two styles of sacrifice bunts: the square around and the pivot in stance.

The Square Around

Many coaches believe that in a square around bunt the batter gets better coverage of the plate if his bat is in fair territory when the bunt is made. The batter assumes his normal stance and when he decides

Illustration 9-7

to bunt he moves his rear leg up and becomes squared to the pitcher
(Illustration 9-7). His knees are flexed and his arms are extended with
the bat level at the top of the strike zone. As he squares, he slides his
top hand up to about where the label of the bat is, with his fingers on
the bottom of the bat and his thumb on top (Illustration 9-8). Both
eyes are focused on the ball and with both shoulders and hips facing
the pitcher. As the pitch arrives, he tries to "catch the ball" with the
barrel of the bat. Tell the player to think of the barrel of the bat as a
baseball mitt, and when he bunts the ball, "play catch" with it. In
bunting for a sacrifice the hitter does not jab or push at the ball. All he
wants to do is give with the arms as if catching a ball to deaden the

Illustration 9-8

impact where the ball and bat meet. Body positioning, when the ball is coming toward you, is extremely important. The hips and shoulders are square to the pitcher, arms are relaxed and out in front of the body at the top of the strike zone. The top hand slides up the bat and the knees are slightly bent and both eyes are focused on the pitcher.

Bat and Ball Contact in Bunting

As stated before, the eyes are focused on the ball with the arms relaxed and extended out at the top of the strike zone (Illustration 9-9). If the pitch is above the bat, let it go. It is very important to bunt pitches only in the strike zone. If the pitch is lower than the bat, go down by flexing the knees to where the pitch is. The bat must be kept level so when the ball is bunted it will go into the ground. If the bottom hand gets higher than the top hand, the chance of the ball being popped up is greater. If the ball is to be bunted toward the third base side, the top hand remains stationary while the bottom hand is pulled back slightly causing the barrel of the bat to face toward third base. If the ball is to be bunted toward the first base side, the bottom hand is pushed slightly forward which faces the barrel of the bat toward first base. Some coaches teach a slight upward tilt of the bat on contact. This is where the barrel of the bat is slightly above the handle giving the ball a better chance of being bunted down (angular bunting). The most important point is to give or "catch" the ball with the bat in order to deaden the impact of the ball, rather than push or jab at it.

Illustration 9-9

The Pivot-In-Stance Method of Bunting (Photo 9-4)

The pivot-in-stance method of bunting is where the batter assumes his normal batting stance and when he is ready to bunt he pivots his body by turning his shoulders and hips square to the pitcher with his arms out in front. The pivot is done by just pivoting on the balls of the feet to square the upper body toward the pitcher. The advantage of this method of bunting is that it allows the batter to "fake bunt" and slash, and it also keeps the catcher back deeper in the catcher's box. The actual bunting technique is the same as the square around method. The arms are extended in the top part of the strike zone and the ball is bunted by just catching it with the bat.

Photo 9-4

Bunting for a Base Hit

The purpose of this bunt is to surprise the defense by placing the ball down on the ground and beating the throw to first. The hitter does not commit himself until the last instant and he either drags or pushes the bunt for a hit. This tactic is used when the third baseman or first baseman is deep in position and the batter bunts the ball between them and the pitcher. If a batter has the ability to bunt for a base hit, he will force the defense to cheat "in" and open more areas for him to hit the ball past the infielders.

Right-Handed Batter Push Bunt

The ball is bunted down the first base side of the diamond. The bunt is directed toward the left side of the pitcher, aiming the ball between the pitcher and first and second base. The batter takes a short lead step with his left (front) foot and meets the ball with the bat aiming in that direction.

Right-Handed Batter Drag Bunt (Illustration 9-10)

This is used when the third baseman is playing deep and the batter wants to direct the ball down the third base line. The batter steps backward with his right foot and shifts his weight to his left foot. The arms extend so that the top of the bat is toward first base and the handle of the bat is slid between the hitter's right side and right elbow just above the right hip. When the bunt is actually made, the weight is shifted back to the rear foot allowing the batter to get out of the batter's box with the right foot.

Illustration 9-10

Left-Handed Batter Drag Bunt (Illustration 9-11)

This is used when the first baseman is playing deep. The ball should be bunted to the left of the pitcher and past him so that the first and second baseman have to field the ball. The batter steps toward the ball with his right foot and tries to meet the ball while his left foot is crossing over the right foot before it hits the ground.

Illustration 9-11

BUNTING DRILLS

Bunting During Batting Practice

Each player should practice bunts during batting practice. Before he takes his regular swings, he should bunt the ball down the first base line and then down the third base line as if it were a sacrifice situation. The next bunt should be an attempt for a base hit using either a drag bunt or push bunt. This procedure should be done each time he bats when taking batting practice.

Bucket Drill

Two buckets are placed on the infield diamond. One down the first base side and the other down the third base side. The batter gets in the batter's box and gets ten bunts. The object is to try and bunt the ball in the buckets or anywhere close to them. The coach can move the buckets to any part of the infield. This drill helps the bunter to concentrate on getting the ball down to a specific area in the infield.

Bunting with the Top Half of the Bat Removed

The top half of a wooden bat is sawed off and the lower half is used for bunting the ball. The batter uses his regular bunting technique to lay down a sacrifice bunt. By having the top part of the bat removed, the batter must concentrate on making contact with the ball on the bottom half of the bat. This makes his chances of bunting the ball on the ground that much greater.

USING FILMS TO IMPROVE YOUR HITTING: A CHECKLIST FOR PLAYERS

The use of video tapes are helpful for the hitter to analyze his hitting mechanics. The following is a checklist that will give hitters a systematic way of looking at these films.

1. Look at your feet first.

——— Is your stride either too long or too short?

——— Is your front foot planted just seconds before you hit the ball?

——— Do you commit your stride way too soon and become a lunge hitter?

——— Is your back foot still planted when you hit the ball?

——— Do you rotate your hips?

2. Then look at your hands and arms.

——— Do you swing the bat at arms length?

——— Does the end of the bat move first or do your hands come forward first?

——— Are your arms, hands, and wrists lazy? No snap in your swing?

——— Do you possess lost motion of the bat before you start your swing, such as a hitch?

——— Do you drive your forward shoulder into ball or pull away?

3. *Watch your head.*

——— Do you keep your head still when swinging, or turn it away before you make contact with ball?

——— Is your head turned enough to get a good look at all pitches with both eyes?

By the use of films, you can judge many things in a hitter. The most important is bat speed. If the hitter has good bat speed, he should be a good hitter and a hitter with power. Listed below are the advantages of a speedy bat:

- A player can pull the good fast ball.
- A player can wait longer to start his swing and won't be prone to swing at as many bad pitches.
- The player's hitting power is increased by a speedy bat.
- A player with a quick bat will not tend to overstride or pull away from pitches as readily as the player with a slower bat.
- A player that has a quick bat has good wrist action which is the essence of a good power hitter.

TIPS FOR HITTERS

1. Select a bat that's comfortable and that you can control.
2. Grip the bat comfortably and firmly, not tensely or tightly.
3. Grip the bat in the fingers, not back in the palms.
4. Assume a comfortable stance that keeps you balanced at all times.
5. Distribute your weight evenly and on the balls of your feet.
6. Keep the head stationary with your eyes on the pitcher and ball.

7. Keep the hips and shoulders level with the front hip and shoulder pointed at the pitcher.

8. Bend the knees slightly to help you relax.

9. Whip the head of the bat into the hitting spot with the arms away from the body and extended.

10. Take a stride which avoids letting the body go too far forward.

11. Open the hips to let the body momentum and power come forward into the swing.

12. After the hips and wrist whip through the ball, let the bat follow completely through.

13. Stay on balance throughout the entire hitting action.

14. Swing at balls only in the strike zone.

15. Always look for your pitch and take advantage of it.

ORGANIZING CONSTRUCTIVE TEAM PRACTICES: How to Schedule the Most Out of Your Daily Workouts

10

Nothing is more boring than a team practice where most of the players stand around doing nothing constructive. A well-organized practice gets all the team members involved in using the skills that are essential during a game situation. The players must know what they are to do at all times so there is no waste during the session. Use the following plan as a guideline for preparing a daily practice that suits *your* team's needs.

TYPICAL PLAN FOR A DAILY PRACTICE SESSION

2:00 P.M.   Each player is on the field ready for practice.

2:00–2:20 P.M. Players are in the outfield doing stretching exercises.

2:20–2:25 P.M. All players take two laps around the field.

2:25–2:35 P.M. Players play catch using their throwing and catching skills.

Outfielders practice the throws they will use in a game. They should grip the ball across the seams and throw it over the top.

Pitchers practicing balance in their delivery by pausing in their pivot before they throw to one another.

Infielders practice getting the ball away quickly and using quick, snappy throws.

2:35–2:50 P.M.   Players work on individual position practice.

The *first baseman* works around the bag, practicing short hops and the switching of his feet on throws to his left and right. Another player stands about 30 feet away, throwing balls in the dirt or to either side of the bag while the first baseman reacts to each situation.

Middle infielders practice double plays. Shortstop and second baseman are in double-play depth, while a pitcher stands just behind the mound and rolls a ball to either player. Whoever receives the ball will practice his feeds while the other infielder practices his pivot.

The *third baseman* practices slow rollers and tags. A pitcher, manager, or coach rolls slow ground balls down the third base line while the third baseman charges and makes the correct move in fielding the ball to throw the runner out. After doing about 10 or 15 of these plays, he then goes to the bag and receives throws practicing his tags.

Catchers work on blocking balls in the dirt. The catchers put full equipment on and have someone throw balls in the dirt right in front of home plate. The catcher practices blocking the ball and keeping it in front so a runner cannot score from third.

Outfielders work on fly balls and grounders. Two pitchers hit fly balls and ground balls to the outfielders while they practice catching the ball on their throwing side and moving in toward the ball. They also practice coming in on grounders and moving to their left and right on both fly balls and ground balls.

Each player on the team has a role in what to do during this individual practice session. It gets everyone moving, while at the same time they are doing work on individual skills.

2:50–3:05 P.M.   Pitchers work on mound drills. The object of these mound drills is to put every pitcher through every situation he would encounter as a fifth infielder. All the pitchers line up behind one another on the mound, each one with a ball in his hand. The infielders go to their positions and the coach is at home plate with a fungo bat ready to hit the ball. The pitchers go through the following situations as they throw the ball home:

- Covering first base on a ground ball hit to the right side.
- The comeback double play.
- Covering first base on a 3-6-1 double play.
- Home to first base double play on a ball hit back to the pitcher.
- Covering sacrifice bunts with a man on first or with a man on second.

As the pitchers and infielders are going through these drills the outfielders are playing pepper to develop hand and eye coordination and agility.

3:05–3:20 P.M.   Players practice defensing the first and third situations and rundowns, using the outfielders as base runners.

3:20–3:30 P.M.   Players practice relays and cutoffs.

3:30 P.M.
to end of
practice

Concentrate on batting practice. Batting can be set up many different ways. Each hitter can take a specified amount of swings. Each group can be given a time limit, or even a game situation can be used.

As batting practice is going on, pitchers should be hitting ground balls to the infielders. Stations can be set up for the on-deck batters where they can be hitting off a "tee" and taking soft tosses.

At the very end of practice you can use a good conditioning drill where your players can run around the bases, to build up their wind and to practice the correct baserunning procedure.

At St. John's we have an extensive fall baseball program where we play over forty games. Since this situation does not allow us to practice once we start playing our games, we must try and keep our nonstarters sharp throughout the season. There is a large area in foul territory by our bullpen. It is in this area that various drills are done by infielders, outfielders, and pitchers who are not in the game.

Infielders take ground balls and work on their fielding and throwing mechanics. A fungo hitter hits ground balls at the infielder as well as to either side. The infielder fields the ball and throws the ball back to a pitcher who is shagging for the fungo hitter.

Outfielders are stationed at a fence taking soft tosses, which helps them to work on their hitting mechanics.

Pitchers are working on their pickoff moves to all bases or doing some throwing in between starts to remain sharp.

After about fifteen minutes, the infielders switch to taking soft tosses and the outfielders take ground balls, working on their scoop play and crow hop after fielding a ground ball.

The coach must set up this schedule and show his players how it is to be done. Once the players are exposed to these drills, they can go down the foul line and do the drills by themselves. This also helps players who enter a game in the late innings to be warmed up properly and ready to go.

TIPS FOR ORGANIZING
A CONSTRUCTIVE TEAM PRACTICE

1. A daily practice schedule should be posted before practice starts.
2. Each practice should have all team members involved in using the skills that are essential during a game situation.
3. During batting practice ground balls should be hit by pitchers or coaches to infielders as well as fly balls to the outfielders.
4. Practice can also be used as a conditioning for your team.
5. Remember to practice the way you *play*.
6. Keep practices moving.

SAFETY MEASURES: Conditioning and Injury Prevention

11

CONDITIONING:
A THREE-STAGE PREVENTIVE PROGRAM

The proper conditioning of the players before the actual season begins will preclude and reduce the chances of many of the typical injuries incurred in baseball. Conditioning also improves the speed, agility, timing, and reflexes used in the sport. We utilize a three-stage program of conditioning for our players: pre-season, in-season, and off-season. Each period has different goals and routines to keep our athletes in shape.

Pre-season

Our pre-season program is done mostly indoors using sneakers or running shoes. Our sessions last between two to three hours in length and are evenly divided between flexibility stretching, running for both speed and endurance, light throwing, easy fielding and hitting, and teaching of proper baseball skills. Three times a week the players will either hit in the indoor cages or throw in our basketball arena. On their alternate days they are encouraged to do circuit training in our weight training room under the supervision of the coach and trainer. This will help increase their muscular strength and endurance for the regular season.

In-season

Our in-season program entails a period of twenty minutes of flexibility stretching, followed by five minutes of running to get our leg muscles loose. Players run from the right field foul line toward center field and back, gradually increasing the speed from an easy jog to speed work. Make sure on colder, windy days that you give the players more time to stretch and warm up before they go into their throwing and infield drills.

Off-season

Our off-season program consists of weight training three times a week along with some type of cardiovascular workout such as racquetball, swimming, cycling, and basketball. We monitor the players' weight every two weeks during the off-season to make sure they don't stray too far from their ideal playing weight.

INJURIES: SOME SOBERING STATISTICS

Baseball is not usually a contact sport. In many plays, opposing players avoid touching one another at all, and in other cases contact is unavoidable. The game can be a contact sport on occasion. A catcher and a runner trying to score at home plate may collide with one another, a player running bases and smashing into an infielder in breaking up a double play, or an outfielder crashing into the wall while chasing a long fly ball are examples of how injuries can occur.

In fact, baseball ranks in the top five causes of accidental injuries to the youth of America, topped only by bicycle injuries, stairway falls, lawnmower accidents, and football, according to a recent study. Seventeen million youths play baseball of some type today. In 1982 there were 900,000 baseball-related injuries reported nationwide to hospital emergency rooms. Of course, 54 percent were contusions or bruises, abrasions or cuts; 24 percent were fractured bones or sprains. Many of these resulted from sliding and collisions, which accounted for 10 percent of all injuries.

Batted balls caused 38 percent of reported baseball injuries, with thrown or pitched balls accounting for 22 percent, while catching caused 14 percent. This is not surprising, considering that many pro ballplayers can throw the ball at over 100 mph, and even many Little

Leaguers can pitch the ball at 70 mph. In the major leagues, batted balls travel at close to 120 mph.

The most important way to reduce baseball injuries is to insist that all players wear appropriate equipment. Most ball teams require players to wear all the equipment provided for them during both games and practices. At times, especially in warm weather, players try to do without protective gear. Coaches should be very firm that all players wear all necessary protection at all times.

Coaches should always insist that every player wear a protective batting helmet during batting practice and in games. They should regularly inspect batting helmets and make sure there are no cracks in the exterior part of the shell as well as in the interior closed-cell vinyl. Coaches should insist that catchers wear the new catchers' helmets, along with the highly protective throat protector, which is attached to the mask.

Rubber-spiked shoes should be worn in all youth league programs. This cuts down greatly on the amount of lacerations and abrasions seen in baseball, as well as the amount of knee and ankle injuries caused when the metal spikes get caught in the grass.

The dugouts should always have a screened fence to protect the ballplayers from foul balls and errant throws.

HOW TO PREVENT INJURIES

There are some things that a coach or trainer can recommend to his players that can reduce or lower the incidence of needless and preventable injuries. They should insist that players:

- Always wear clean underclothing for practice and games. Shirts, socks, supporters, and uniforms should be washed daily.
- Change the undershirt (if available) between games of a doubleheader or every four or five innings on hot, humid days.
- Be sure to dress properly for cold weather baseball. Several layers of clothing are better than one heavy garment.
- Don't wear rings, watches or chains/necklaces during games.
- Shower and change immediately after every game or practice. Dry thoroughly before going outside into cool weather.
- Stretch and loosen up thoroughly before every game or practice session.

- Avoid indecision in sliding—once a player has decided either to slide or stay up, he should do so.
- Don't slide head first. The injury rate for players who slide head first is almost ten times the amount of injury to those sliding in feet first.
- Call all fly balls in the infield and outfield.
- Keep all bats in the bat rack where they can't get in the way of play.
- Be sure to have screens in place in front of the batting practice pitcher, the middle infield area behind second base, and first base to protect the players from errant throws and batted balls during batting practice.

A well-equipped medical kit for use for the team should include the following articles:

tape	hydrogen peroxide
roller gauze	tape adherent
ace bandages	petroleum jelly
band aids	penlight
foam	baby powder
felt	eye wash
aspirin	linament
antacid tablets	throat lozenges
butterfly closures	shoe laces
bacitracin ointment	eye black sun-glare
ice bags	mirror
tongue depressors	scissors
gauze pads	thermometer
finger splints	

Index